Children's Libraries

Children's Libraries

Anne Fleet, A.L.A.

 ANDRE DEUTSCH/A Grafton Book

First published 1973 by
André Deutsch Limited
105 Great Russell Street London WC1

Copyright © 1973 Anne Fleet
All rights reserved

Printed in Great Britain by
Ebenezer Baylis and Son Limited
The Trinity Press, Worcester, and London

ISBN 0 233 96229 8

Contents

List of figures

Preface

This book is an attempt to cover the field of children's library work in public libraries with particular emphasis on conditions in Britain. It was decided to omit the history of children's libraries as this has been ably covered by Alec Ellis in his articles in the *Library Association Record* and *Journal of Librarianship*. I hope that I have managed to impart some of the pleasure and joy that I have experienced from working with children and books in libraries.

I hope my male colleagues will bear with me in that I have generally referred to children's librarians in the feminine. This is a matter of convenience as at present the majority are women although I hope there will be a more balanced proportion in the future.

I am extremely grateful for the help and encouragement I have received from my former chief, Mr K. C. Harrison, the City Librarian of Westminster, and to Jennifer Shepherd, Assistant County Librarian, Children and Youth, Leicestershire County Library, and Marie Le Comte, District Children's Librarian, Westminster City Libraries, who read and made such helpful comments on the manuscript. It is impossible to mention all the individuals and libraries from whom I received information or visited informally but I should like to especially mention the staff of the International Youth Library, the National Library for the Blind, Leicestershire, and the West Sussex County Libraries who so generously gave of their time to help me, and Bibliotekscentralen, Denmark, for their long and informative answer to my enquiry. I am also indebted to the staff of the Library Association Library for all their help, to *Library and Information Science Abstracts* and to David Lewis of Westminster City Libraries who obtained for me so many relevant pamphlets and books from the staff library.

My grateful thanks to Patricia Davenport and Patricia Ryan who typed the manuscript and bibliographies respectively and finally to my husband who showed considerable forbearance during the entire period the manuscript was being written.

ANNE FLEET *February* 1972

Chapter 1
The Child's Need for Books

I like books that remain faithful to the very essence of art; namely, those that offer to children an intuitive and direct way of knowledge, a simple beauty capable of being perceived immediately, arousing in their souls a vibration that will endure all their lives.

PAUL HAZARD, *Books, Children and Men*[1]

This quotation sums up what we, the middlemen, whether as teachers, librarians, reviewers, booksellers or publishers, should be striving to find and introduce to children and their parents; literature that will enrich the imagination, the intellect, and will be an experience in their lives.

Defining a children's book is difficult and sometimes impossible. Authors of high calibre usually write for themselves without an age group in mind, and it is left to publishers to decide whether to put the book on their adult or children's list. Sometimes librarians refuse to place books which will be enjoyed equally by adults and children in both stocks. *The Owl Service* by Alan Garner, for example, is appreciated by children and many adults, as are the books of Hester Burton. Books not originally written for children, e.g. *Robinson Crusoe, Gulliver's Travels*, and the novels of Dickens, have been adopted by children. For our purpose a children's book is one that children will read, enjoy and probably return to later, whether it was intended originally for them or one that they have taken for their own. Such a book is judged on the same literary criteria as all other works, and if it is literature in its own right the adult reader as well as the child will lose himself in the book, and the plot and characters will be alive in his imaginative thoughts thereafter.

The child's imagination is fired by entering the realm of books. A thoughtful mother will expose her child to the rhythm of words and songs from the earliest years. Three excellent books immediately come to mind – *Lavender's Blue* by Kathleen

Lines, *This Little Pig Went to Market* by Norah Montgomerie, and *This Little Puffin* by Elizabeth Matterson. These show nursery rhymes, finger plays and actions for nursery rhymes to play with a baby. Paul Hazard describes the English nursery rhyme as the poetry of childhood, uniting our people together, wherever they may be, and shows that without this background Englishmen do not completely understand each other. The child hearing the same rhymes again and again will later gradually join in. It is known that the formative years of a child's life before he reaches school are the most important of all. Activities are now held, particularly in the United States but also in parts of Britain, to give the deprived child the opportunity through participation in play, toys, books and varying visits to develop to his own capabilities so that he does not enter school at an educational as well as a social disadvantage.

The young child is very receptive and uninhibited, but many children today suffer severe limitations in their environment. In our cities many children live in blocks of flats, only a few have play areas on some floors, and frequently the child cannot play outside because the mother is too far away to keep watch and do her work at the same time. Playing with clay, sand or water is too messy to do indoors. A story hour in the library for children under five may be a godsend to the mother, especially if the period is set completely aside for young children. She will not be embarrassed if her offspring is lively, and together they will be able to choose books to take home afterwards. The child has need of very simple books at first. A toddler will enjoy *I See a Lot of Things* by Dean Hay, an attractive collection of photographs of nursery objects. You can watch the young child try to pick up a figure in a picture and clutch it in the same way as he will lift up his toys. Very occasionally we are asked for rag books in our libraries, but apart from aesthetic or more practical considerations these are not a good proposition from an hygienic point of view. The child has 'insatiable curiosity' and is anxious to learn about his own surroundings, and others less familiar. Through picture books his imagination will be stretched and he will gain new experiences from his everyday life, and eventually travel to far-off places – the Land of Babar, of Ping, Madeline and Anatole. It may be more successful if at first the child is introduced to a story in a setting more like his home. *Angus Lost*, for example, in which a little Scottie dog becomes curious and runs away. *Teddy Bear Coalman* is another favourite and *The Elephant and the Bad Baby* is superb. The elephant takes the baby to see all the shopkeepers a small child will be familiar with, and takes of their wares, but the baby always forgets to say please. All the shopkeepers follow them home and Mother makes pancakes for everyone.

It is very rewarding to watch young children choose their books. Instinctively they appear to pick out the best, with pictures which are beautifully drawn, and tell a story, as in *Borka*, or *Mike Mulligan and His Steam Shovel*. The type of picture book which is precocious or cute to lure adults into purchasing it as a present is often rejected. The child appears to recognize the insensitivity and condescension to childhood characteristic of them. Young children enjoy the alphabet books, and Brian Wildsmith's, John Burningham's or Robert Broomfield's *Baby Animal A.B.C.* are invaluable. Tribute must be paid in the nursery rhyme section to the work of Raymond Briggs and *The Mother Goose Treasury* is a book which ideally should be available in every home. Artistic interpretations of single, well-known nursery rhymes are also available, such as *London Bridge Is Falling Down* by Peter Spier and *Old Mother Hubbard and Her Dog* by Paul Galdone.

Special books are necessary for Christmas and other occasions. Good picture books include *Away in a Manger*, *The Little Drummer Boy* and *Christmas in the Stable*. For story-telling, Ruth Sawyer's *The Long Christmas* is invaluable, and Ezra Keats's *The Snowy Day* imparts the joy of snow for the first time. *Peter's Chair* by the same author is very reassuring to the small child who may feel his belongings are being taken away for a young brother or sister.

A few library authorities do not allow children to join the library in their own right while under school age. The reason given is that the provision of picture books is too expensive, and sometimes that children cannot read. Parents should refuse to accept such rulings and the need to get around them by using their own tickets and depriving themselves of books. It is essential that dissatisfaction should be expressed by individuals to the authority concerned, and if this fails through the local press or organizations like the Federation of Children's Book Groups. Childhood should be rich both educationally and socially to develop the child to his full potential. Success in our world depends largely on literacy. In the future much of the non-skilled work will be done more economically by machines, and we will be in need of greater education in the work we do. We shall have to know how to find information, and where to go for help. Increased leisure and a longer life-span will result in an even greater need for recreational, social and educational activities outside our normal work. It is never too early to expose children to the pleasure of books and reading to give them happier and more fulfilled lives.

Parents sometimes leave young children in the children's library while they choose their own books. I shall always remember a little boy about four years old, called Johnnie. There was a slope in the East York Library, near Toronto, where the child could rest his book while sitting down on a bench and turning the pages. The book he was 'reading' was *Madeline and the Gypsies*. Through the pictures of Madeline, Pepito, the gypsies and the circus, he was telling himself out loud an adventure story. I was so fascinated that I sat still, rooted to my desk, and hoped that no one would come in to disturb him. The pictures are gay and humorous and tell the story beautifully and Johnnie at this stage would probably not have appreciated a straight reading of the text anyway.

Frequently we are asked by mothers, 'Which books do you think he will enjoy?' We need more books which are imaginative, with a simple text for the parent to read, a plot capable of being understood by a young child and a central character the child may identify himself with. Pictures should be well drawn and portray the entire story with more detail than the text. The pictures must be lively and, like the text, have a definite beginning, middle and end. An excellent book to give a mother starting to read books to her child is *Harry, the Dirty Dog* by Gene Zion. Parents, playgroup leaders, and the matrons of day nurseries discuss, sometimes at great length, the type of illustrations children like in books from our libraries. We hear whether or not they like highly coloured illustrations like those by Brian Wildsmith. Some prefer soft pastel shades or pictures in two or three tones. It is probably true on the whole that children prefer coloured pictures, but *Choo, Choo* by V. L. Burton and *The Story of Ferdinand* by Munro Leaf are notable exceptions. We ask that children be given the books to look at themselves and some which are criticized by adults return obviously well used by the children.

Picture books cover a wide age range. The younger children will have them read aloud, but children in the infant school and even in the junior school will enjoy reading them until they have acquired a fairly fluent reading ability. Children of different ages enjoy the same books, except those obviously intended for a baby. Older children will appreciate the following books more than the younger ones, particularly if the books are introduced to a group, although an individual younger child may well enjoy them. *The Story of Horace* by Alice M. Coats is popular; children laugh excitedly at the pictures, hardly able to wait for the pages to be turned to see who is now missing, and joining in the cumulative text. *Joseph's Yard* and other picture books by Charles Keeping portray city life with an exciting use of colour in the pictures. In *Where the Wild Things Are* by Maurice Sendak, the 'Wild Things' are grotesque and many adults feared children would be frightened but they are not, because Max, the boy, is always in complete control. Children create their own rumpuses of the 'Wild Things'; one infants' school prepared a dance and many schools entered a painting competition organized by the publishers, The Bodley Head.

There are some beautiful individual fairy and folk stories and legends such as *The Diverting Adventures of Tom Thumb* illustrated by Barry Wilkinson, and *The Three Little Pigs* illustrated by William Stobbs. Grimms' Tales, *Rapunzel* and *The Seven Ravens*, are illustrated by Felix Hoffman who captures the feeling and mood of the tales; his rather sombre pictures adding to the suspense. Virginia Haviland has retold tales from many countries in such books as *Favourite Fairy Tales Told in Spain* which are useful when the child is unable to tackle more difficult collections and in which the original sources are given. The Bodley Head have another series of fairytales edited by Kathleen Lines, including *Cinderella*, illustrated by Shirley Hughes. Barbara Cooney has retold and drawn tastefully *The Little Juggler* from an old French legend and in this field there is also the work of Brian Wildsmith who illustrated the La Fontaine Fables which appeal to very young children. The text is simple and the pictures of *The Northwind and the Sun* glorious.

Once a child has mastered the mechanics of reading, a new world gradually unfolds, and he may go wherever he wishes. Perhaps into the land of fantasy with *The Lion, the Witch and the Wardrobe* by C. S. Lewis, *Elidor* by Alan Garner and *The Hobbit* by J. R. R. Tolkien, or he may read the magical stories of E. Nesbit. He may go back or forward in time as in *The Ghosts* by Antonia Barber, *The Children of Green Knowe* by Lucy M. Boston, *The Gauntlet* by Ronald Welch which is always enjoyed, in which Peter becomes one of his Norman ancestors in a castle on the Welsh border and which contains an authentic description of a medieval dinner and *A Traveller in Time* by Alison Uttley, in which Penelope finds herself involved in a plot to rescue Mary, Queen of Scots. Sometimes the child prefers humorous stories; examples are *Stuart Little* by E. B. White or *Mr. Popper's Penguins* by Richard and Florence Atwater. History is well represented both factually and in fiction. Hester Burton's novels often ably state the case of those who were persecuted by officialdom in former days, such as the printer who published a tract advocating land ownership by parishes instead of rich landlords in *Time of Trial*. Leon Garfield in *Smith* and *Black Jack* has also written exciting historical novels – Smith's escape from Newgate is masterly. For earlier periods in history *The Dream Time* by Henry Treece is an exceptionally fine book and, as in all of Rosemary Sutcliff's novels, the reader really feels that he is present and involved in the plot. With some books this is prevented by the suspicion that the author is not completely in sympathy or has a lack of real knowledge of the period in which he has rather artificially set his story, or has used language which is inappropriate. Some children enjoy science fiction and André Norton, Peter Dickinson, John Christopher, and of course Jules Verne are firm favourites.

Myths, legends and hero stories should not be forgotten. For a first choice I would give *The Heroes* by Charles Kingsley. Roger Lancelyn Green has made an invaluable contribution with *Old Greek Fairy Tales* and *Heroes of Greece and Troy*, as has Ian Serraillier with *The Gorgon's Head*, the story of Perseus, and *The Way of Danger*, the story of Theseus. For the legends and sagas of Iceland, Allen French provides an excellent introduction with *Grettir The Strong*; Dorothy Hosford's *Thunder of the Gods* is a very readable and moving version of the Norse myths, while *Beowulf* may be found in verse by Ian Serrailler or in prose by Rosemary Sutcliff. Roger Lancelyn Green, Howard Pyle and Barbara Leonie Picard are all responsible for much-loved versions of King Arthur.

Children enjoy poetry from the earliest years. Unfortunately many children are not read to at all, and others have parents who feel it is no longer necessary to read aloud once they can read for themselves. Poetry is very intimate and is most appreciated in the family or with small groups at a story hour. The child needs to hear the beauty of the language and the rhythm of poetry. Two excellent anthologies for young children are Leonard Clark's *Drums and Trumpets* and *Flutes and Cymbals*, while Walter De La Mare's anthologies, *Tom Tiddler's Ground* and *Come Hither*, are excellent presents for a family. Eleanor Graham has chosen poems for *Thread of Gold* and *The Puffin Book of Verse* which are both enjoyed. Funny poems especially to tempt children who shy away from poetry are Hilaire Belloc's *Cautionary Tales for Children*, Edward Lear's *The Jumblies*, and T. S. Eliot's *Old Possum's Book of Practical Cats*. These are but a few of the outstanding books in this field and we must not forget Eleanor Farjeon and James Reeves who have made a consistently fine contribution to the poetry of childhood; and Ian Serrailler who has done likewise with his retelling of Robin Hood in the form of ballads.

Anne Carol Moore, the esteemed American children's librarian and pioneer in the field, feared 'that the commercial production of children's books for profit would result in inferiority, and that children's books might cease to be a contribution to literature'.[2] Cheap, shoddy books of the type Anne Carol Moore feared are not difficult to find and are still being produced. There is, however, a highly responsible body of editors in Japan, the United States, Australia, Europe and Britain, discovering and encouraging new authors and illustrators in our field. Publishers obtain the rights of books to be published by another foreign house, and sometimes the books are published simultaneously in this country and abroad. Many of the beautiful picture books produced today would not be available at their present price if international co-operation did not take place.

In the English-speaking world we are fortunate that a large

proportion of our books are not translated from a foreign language. Danish librarians particularly have spoken of the distortion in the atmosphere and feeling of a book through poor translation. We have been fortunate with the translation of works of authors like René Guillot by Gwen Marsh.

It is distressing today when so many books of high quality are readily available to see the small and often inferior collections in the homes of children. These children are often beautifully dressed and have many toys which they may soon have outgrown and forgotten, yet the books which a child and a whole family could grow up with and later treasure in their own homes and enjoy again with their own children, are missing. Instead the crudely illustrated stereotyped story which does not leave any room for imagination or reflection is represented.

Children unfortunately are rarely given the opportunity to buy their own hardcover books. It is left to parents, friends and relatives, many of whom did not know the pleasure of reading when young, and who appear to have grown up without appreciation and judgement in the choosing of books for children. The tide however is beginning to turn; more adults are reading the books children take home or are borrowing themselves. This has been particularly noticeable in the commuter libraries in central London in recent years. More space is being given in a few of the daily papers to articles and reviews of children's books which have included excellent articles by Brian Alderson in *The Times* and by John Rowe Townsend in the *Guardian*. Articles also appear by critics in the *Sunday Times* and the *Observer* from time to time. However, a good deal more could appear. Articles are written, usually by non-specialists, in the women's pages from time to time. They stir up considerable interest from members of the public, but the approach is more journalistic than critical. One wishes there was more obvious consultation when there is a specialist in the field writing regularly for the newspaper. Parents will find *Children's Book Review*, a bi-monthly publication extremely helpful. There are articles and reviews written by specialists in each number, and the identity of the reviewer is given.

Margery Fisher, literary critic, has also produced *Growing Point*, a critical but fairly chatty review of books for the growing family. Mrs Fisher, awarded the Eleanor Farjeon award in recognition of services to children's literature in 1966, reviews most of the books herself, and one must admire her energy and devotion.

The Children's Book Centre in Kensington Church Street is a delight to both adults and children. Talks by authors, and illustrators' and publishers' weeks are held from time to time. The Rainbow-Bookshop at Walton-on-Thames is also a specialist bookshop for children, and includes a weekly reading club which is periodically visited by authors and illustrators. Other specialist bookshops include Book One in North London, and a children's bookshop at Heffer's in Cambridge.

One of the most interesting developments in recent years has been the evolution of the Federation of Children's Book Groups. Anne Wood started the first Books for Children group in 1965 at Walton-on-Thames. As a teacher in a secondary school she had become aware that many children had been deprived of the joy of reading. Later she recommended books for a paper-back scheme in schools. There are now groups forming all over the country. Her periodical *Books for Your Children* appears four times a year and includes articles on many aspects of children's reading from books for the very young to the teenager. Parents, writers and publishers contribute. Varying activities for parents and children such as talks by authors and publishers, the showing of films, and storytelling are promoted by different groups. Anne Wood was awarded the Eleanor Farjeon award in recognition of her work for books for children in 1968.

The Federation is not primarily a pressure group, but when the Books for Children groups have made efforts to get better provision for children they have not always met with sympathy and help from the libraries concerned. This is deplorable as children's librarians sometimes complain of apathy on the part of parents, and it is any librarian's duty, when there is not a children's librarian, to serve children as ably as any other section of the community.

Many children today are deprived of normal contact through play and participation with other children. As I have previously mentioned, city-living may place severe limitations on the places available for play. It has been suggested that by 1980 children from two years old will be able to attend nursery school. In the Plowden Report it was recommended that part-time nursery education should be available to all children who had reached the age of three at the beginning of the school year until the age for compulsory schooling.[3] Local authorities were entitled to set up nursery schools by the Education Act of 1944, but were subsequently directed not to start any more nursery schools or classes as it was feared that expenditure would be diverted from the infants' schools. There are now more places being provided in educational priority areas, and in others a child will be given a place if the mother can be released for teaching in the schools. Some authorities, including Hertfordshire and the Inner London Education Authority, are more enlightened. Parents and other voluntary bodies became aware that their children needed more stimulation through contact with other children, and formed playgroups. Playgroups are also run by the 'Save the Children Fund', the local Councils of Social Service and by the local authority in clinic premises. Voluntary bodies like health societies and societies for mentally handicapped children and the Children's Invalid Association also run their own playgroups. Some playgroups visit the library for the normal story hour for the under fives, others where the number will be too large or the story hour is at an unsuitable time for them, have their own. Books are chosen for the playgroup, but many of the children return with their mothers to change their own books. Collections of twenty books at a time are also delivered to groups which are normally too far away from a library with facilities to receive a group of children. This service is appreciated, and one is agreeably surprised at how well the children look after the books. Some libraries have display collections which tour around the branch libraries, and playgroup leaders are invited to see them.

The emergence of the paperback has resulted in children being able to buy many more books for themselves. Tribute must be paid to the work of Miss Kaye Webb, to whom the Eleanor Farjeon award has been given, and the staff of Penguin Books Limited who publish the Puffin series for children and the Peacock series for older children. Members receive a badge and the magazine *Puffin Post*. Excellent articles are written by authors and other contributors, there are competitions and opportunities given to meet authors. Authors represented include William Mayne, Leon Garfield, Alan Garner, C. S. Lewis, Rosemary

Sutcliff, and Roger Lancelyn Green. The picture Puffins for the young child are outstanding value and include *Fee, Fi, Fo, Fum* and *The Twelve Days of Christmas*. Methuen have produced the works of A. A. Milne and Faber's paperbacks include Hans Andersen's *Forty-two Stories*, V. L. Burton's *The Little House*, and Walter De La Mare's *Peacock Pie*. Oxford University Press are also publishing their own paperbacks.

The child who is a keen reader is often a member of the Puffin Club already, and is building up his own library. One little girl said she always borrowed the books from the library first to decide whether they were really the books she wanted for her own before spending her pocket money. The less able reader if given the choice will often prefer a paperback. Daniel Fader in his interesting work *Hooked on Books*[4] suggested that hardbacks are associated by some children with failure in school.

Thus it is hoped a child's collection of books will grow and include both those chosen by himself and books of quality chosen by his parents, relatives and friends. These books will become part of his life, always readily available to be read and re-read, or referred to, and will not be discarded like so many of the childhood things he has outgrown if they have been a worthwhile and rewarding experience. Childhood is very short and it is essential that the child should be exposed to all forms of literature appropriate to his stages of development. He will unfortunately, even with a personal collection and a good school or children's library, not have the opportunity to read everything he would enjoy. However, if a habit of reading is established when young, this will continue to enrich his life. Few families will be able to afford to buy all the books needed, or have room to house them in today's modern houses and flats. Many books are only required for a short time, so it is essential that they should be readily available from the library and the school.

It is a statutory duty of local authorities to provide a library service.[5] The service point may be a well-equipped children's room, a section in a small branch, a mobile library, or books may be provided at schools in rural areas. In 1974, with the exception of London, local authority areas are changing[6] so that there will not be the present separation between county and municipal authorities. These larger units should result in a better and more even service throughout the country.

REFERENCES

1 Paul Hazard. *Books, Children and Men.* 4th edition. Boston, The Horn Book, 1960.
2 Anne Carol Moore. *My Roads to Childhood : Views and Reviews of Children's Books.* New edition. Boston, The Horn Book, 1961.
3 Department of Education and Science. *Children and Their Primary Schools. A Report of the Central Advisory Council for Education (England) Volume I* (Plowden Report). London, HMSO, 1961.
4 Daniel Fader. *Hooked on Books.* Oxford, Pergamon Press, 1966.
5 Public Libraries and Museum Act, 1964, ch. 75. London, HMSO, 1964.
6 Royal Commission on Local Government in England (Redcliffe-Maude Report). London, HMSO, 1969.

FURTHER READING

Eyre, Frank. *British Children's Books in the Twentieth Century.* London, Longman, 1971.
Fenwick, Sara Innis. (ed.). *A Critical Approach to Children's Literature : the Thirty-First Annual Conference of the Graduate Library School. August 1–3. 1966.* Chicago and London, University of Chicago Press, 1967.
Fisher, Margery. 'Children's Fiction As Literature'. *Proceedings of the Llandudno Conference, 1962.* London, Library Association, 1962.
Fisher, Margery. *Intent Upon Reading : A Critical Appraisal of Modern Fiction for Children.* 2nd edition. London, Brockhampton, 1964.
Hurlimann, Bettina. *Picture-Book World.* Translated and edited by Brian W. Alderson. London, Oxford University Press, 1968.
Keeping, Charles. 'Conveying A Fresh Vision'. *Books and Bookmen,* May 1970. pp. 30–2.
Macrae, Julia. 'Is Blandness Creeping In'. *Top of the News,* vol. 25, no. 3, April 1969. pp. 252–5. (A possible danger in publishing books for an international market.)
Meigs, Cornelia; Eaton, Anne Thaxter; Nesbitt, Elizabeth, and Viguers, Ruth Hill. *A Critical History of Children's Literature : A Survey of Children's Books in English.* Prepared in four parts under the editorship of Cornelia Meigs. Revised edition. New York, Collier-Macmillan, 1969.
Smith, Lillian H. *The Unreluctant Years : A Critical Approach to Children's Literature.* Chicago, American Library Association, 1953.
Townsend, John Rowe. 'The Present State of English Children's Literature'. *Wilson Library Bulletin,* vol. 43, October 1968. pp. 126–32.
Viguers, Ruth Hill. *Margin for Surprise : About Books, Children and Librarians.* London, Constable Young Books, 1966.
White, Dorothy. *About Books for Children.* New York, Oxford University Press, 1949.
White, Dorothy. *Books Before Five.* Wellington, New Zealand Council for Educational Research, 1954.
'A Valid Criticism for Children's Books'. *Wilson Library Bulletin,* no. 44, December 1969. pp. 394–457.

RECOMMENDED BOOKS

Aiken, Joan. *Night Birds on Nantucket*. London, Cape, 1966.
Andersen, Hans Christian. *Forty-Two Stories*. London, Faber, 1968.
Atwater, Richard and Florence. *Mr. Popper's Penguins*. London, The Bodley Head, 1962.
Barber, Antonia. *The Ghosts*. London, Cape, 1969.
Belloc, Hilaire. *Cautionary Tales for Children*. London, Duckworth, 1960.
Bemelmans, Ludwig. *Madeline and the Gypsies*. London, André Deutsch, 1956.
Boston, Lucy M. *The Children of Green Knowe*. London, Faber, 1954.
Briggs, Raymond. *Fee Fi Fo Fum*. Picture Puffins for the Very Young. Harmondsworth, Penguin, 1969. Also available in hardback, London, Hamish Hamilton, 1964.
Briggs, Raymond. *The Mother Goose Treasury*. London, Hamish Hamilton, 1966.
Broomfield, Robert. *Baby Animal ABC*. Picture Puffins for the Very Young. Harmondsworth, Penguin, 1970. Also available in hardback, London, The Bodley Head, 1964.
Broomfield, Robert. *The Twelve Days of Christmas*. Picture Puffins for the Very Young. Harmondsworth, Penguin, 1968. Also available in hardback, London, The Bodley Head, 1965.
Burningham, John. *ABC*. London, Cape, 1964.
Burningham, John. *Borka*. London, Cape, 1963.
Burton, Hester. *Time of Trial*. London, Oxford University Press, 1963.
Burton, Virginia Lee. *Choo-Choo : The Story of A Little Engine Who Ran Away*. London, Faber, 1967.
Burton, Virginia Lee. *The Little House*. London, Faber, 1968.
Christopher, John. *The White Mountains*. London, Hamish Hamilton, 1967. First of trilogy.
Clark, Leonard. *Drums and Trumpets*. London, The Bodley Head, 1962.
Clark, Leonard. *Flutes and Cymbals*. London, The Bodley Head, 1968.
Coats, Alice M. *The Story of Horace*. London, Faber, 1937.
Cooney, Barbara. *The Little Juggler*. London, Longmans Young Books, 1961.
Defoe, Daniel. *Robinson Crusoe*. Children's Illustrated Classics. London, Dent, 1958.
Dickinson, Peter. *The Weathermonger*. London, Gollancz, 1968.
Eliot, T. S. *Old Possum's Book of Practical Cats*. Illustrated by Nicholas Bentley. London, The Bodley Head, 1955.
Flack, Marjorie. *Angus Lost*. London, The Bodley Head, 1970.
French, Allen. *Grettir the Strong*. London, The Bodley Head, 1961.
Galdone, Paul. *Old Mother Hubbard and Her Dog*. London, The Bodley Head, 1961.
Garfield, Leon. *Black Jack*. London, Longmans Young Books, 1968.
Garfield, Leon. *Smith*. London, Longmans Young Books, 1967.
Garner, Alan. *Elidor*. London, Collins, 1965.
Garner, Alan. *The Owl Service*. London, Collins, 1967.
Graham, Eleanor. *The Puffin Book of Verse*. Harmondsworth, Penguin, 1969.
Graham, Eleanor. *Thread of Gold*. London, The Bodley Head, 1964.

Green, Roger Lancelyn. *Heroes of Greece and Troy*. London, The Bodley Head, 1960.

Green, Roger Lancelyn. *King Arthur and His Knights of the Round Table*. London, Faber, 1957.

Green, Roger Lancelyn. *Old Greek Fairy Tales*. London, Bell, 1958.

Grimm, J. L. and W. K. *Rapunzel*. Illustrated by Felix Hoffmann. London, Oxford University Press, 1961.

Grimm, J. L. and W. K. *The Seven Ravens*. Illustrated by Felix Hoffmann. London, Oxford University Press, 1963.

Guillot, René. *Sama*. Translated by Gwen Marsh. London, Oxford University Press, 1966.

Haviland, Virginia. *Favourite Fairy Tales Told in Spain*. London, The Bodley Head, 1966.

Hay, Dean. *I See A Lot of Things*. London, Collins, 1966.

Hosford, Dorothy. *Thunder of the Gods*. London, The Bodley Head, 1964.

Keats, Ezra Jack. *The Little Drummer Boy*. London, The Bodley Head, 1969.

Keats, Ezra Jack. *Peter's Chair*. London, The Bodley Head, 1968.

Keats, Ezra Jack. *The Snowy Day*. London, The Bodley Head, 1967.

Keeping, Charles. *Joseph's Yard*. London, Oxford University Press, 1969.

Kingsley, Charles. *The Heroes*. Children's Illustrated Classics. London, Dent, 1964.

La Fontaine, Jean de. *The North Wind and the Sun*. Illustrated by Brian Wildsmith. London, Oxford University Press, 1964.

Leaf, Munro. *The Story of Ferdinand*. London, Hamish Hamilton, 1967.

Lear, Edward. *The Jumblies and Other Nonsense Verses*. Illustrated by Leslie L. Brooke. London, Warne, 1968.

Lewis, C. S. *The Lion, the Witch and the Wardrobe*. London, Bles, 1950.

Lindgren, Astrid. *Christmas in the Stable*. London, Brockhampton, 1963.

Lines, Kathleen. *Lavender's Blue*. London, Oxford University Press, 1959.

Mare, Walter de la. *Come Hither*. London, Longmans Young Books, 1960.

Mare, Walter de la. *Peacock Pie*. London, Faber, 1969.

Mare, Walter de la. *Tom Tiddler's Ground*. London, The Bodley Head, 1961.

Matterson, Elizabeth. *This Little Puffin*. Harmondsworth, Penguin, 1969.

Milne, A. A. *The World of Pooh*. Illustrated by E. H. Shepard. London, Methuen, 1958.

Montgomerie, Norah. *This Little Pig Went to Market*. London, The Bodley Head, 1966.

Nesbit, E. *Five Children and It*. London, Benn, 1957.

Norton, André. *Star Guard*. London, Gollancz, 1955.

Nussbaumer, Mares and Paul. *Away in A Manger*. London, Longmans Young Books, 1965.

Perrault, Charles. *Cinderella*. Illustrated in colour by Shirley Hughes. Fairy Tale Picture Books. London, The Bodley Head, 1970.

Picard, Barbara Leonie. *Stories of King Arthur and His Knights*. Oxford Illustrated Classics. London, Oxford University Press, 1965.

Pyle, Howard. *The Story of King Arthur and His Knights*. New York, Dover, 1966.

Sawyer, Ruth. *The Long Christmas*. London, The Bodley Head, 1964.

Sendak, Maurice. *Where the Wild Things Are*. London, The Bodley Head, 1967.

Serrailler, Ian. *Beowulf – the Warrior*. London, Oxford University Press, 1954.

Serrailler, Ian. *The Challenge of the Green Knight*. London, Oxford University Press, 1966.

Serrailler, Ian. *The Gorgon's Head*. London, Oxford University Press, 1961.

Serrailler, Ian. *Robin in the Greenwood*. London, Oxford University Press, 1967.

Serrailler, Ian. *The Way of Danger*. London, Oxford University Press, 1962.

Spier, Peter. *London Bridge Is Falling Down*. Mother Goose Library. Tadworth, World's Work, 1968.

Stobbs, William. *The Story of the Three Little Pigs*. London, The Bodley Head, 1968.

Sutcliff, Rosemary. *The Eagle of the Ninth*. London, Oxford University Press, 1954.

Sutcliff, Rosemary. *Beowulf*. London, The Bodley Head, 1961.

Swift, Jonathan. *Gulliver's Travels*. Oxford Illustrated Classics. London, Oxford University Press, 1955.

Tolkien, J. R. R. *The Hobbit*. London, Allen and Unwin, 1966.

Treece, Henry. *The Dream-time*. London, Brockhampton, 1967.

Uttley, Alison. *A Traveller in Time*. London, Faber, 1939.

Verne, Jules. *Around the Moon*. Children's Illustrated Classics. London, Dent, 1970.

Verne, Jules. *From the Earth to the Moon*. Children's Illustrated Classics. London, Dent, 1970.

Vipont, Elfrida, and Briggs, Raymond. *The Elephant and the Bad Baby*. London, Hamish Hamilton, 1969.

Welch, Ronald. *The Gauntlet*. Oxford Children's Library. London, Oxford University Press, 1958.

White, E. B. *Stuart Little*. London, Hamish Hamilton, 1946.

Wildsmith, Brian. *ABC*. London, Oxford University Press, 1962.

Wilkinson, Barry. *The Diverting Adventures of Tom Thumb*. London, The Bodley Head, 1967.

Worthington, Phoebe and Selby. *Teddy Bear Coalman*. London, Warne, 1948.

Chapter 2
Planning New Libraries

The site of any library is of first importance, but before a site is selected it must be decided who the library is going to serve and what services are desirable to meet the needs of the community. A basic principle is that a building must be planned from within to without. Every head of department must assess how much space is required now, and how much will be required as the community changes. Are there any large-scale housing developments? If so, are they public, by housing associations or private, and in what category, luxury or more modest accommodation? Are new schools planned? Are they to replace existing schools and if so how many places will they have? Is the small town becoming a natural centre for the country around? Is the present centre of the town changing? Are popular stores like Marks & Spencer, Woolworths, Sainsbury's coming in or moving to a new site? Is new industry coming into the town? When determining the spatial requirement the children's librarian will have to consider whether the children's library should be separate, whether charging is to be done in the children's room or centrally for all readers, and whether lectures are to be given there or if a lecture hall could be justified. Is a homework area necessary? Is it possible to cut off part of the children's library for a story hour or class visit without depriving other readers of the opportunity to borrow books, or do you need an activities room? The proximity of the workroom to the children's library will have to be considered when the relationship of departments is being planned on a known site, but at the earliest stage sufficient space should be allowed for a workroom which is adjacent. Will the children's librarian in this building be in charge or responsible for the training of staff, or will it be necessary for her to interview teachers, booksellers, publishers and prospective members of staff? If this is the case, a combined office and workroom shared by all members of the children's staff will not ensure sufficient privacy and an office should be provided. The children's librarian will need to liaise with other departmental heads, for such facilities as an auditorium, lecture halls and exhibition areas to be used by all services. All concerned should read the council and committee reports of other departments to seek any relevant information on new housing, slum clearance, new roads, new schools, play centres and special schools for mentally handicapped children. The chief and deputy librarian will co-ordinate the proposed requirements making necessary adjustments and alterations and allowing extra room for circulation. They will often have worked out spatial requirements for the total building and individual departments. This practice serves as a double check, and also gives individual departmental heads the opportunity to state their aims and needs for the particular section of the community that they are directly concerned with.

A poor site can result in the loss of fifty per cent of total use – libraries should not be set in parks, side streets or civic centres unless the latter are the natural centre of the town. Many people combine a visit to the library with shopping. Children often go swimming at nearby baths before they change their books. There are other problems to be considered. Is there adequate, free car-parking space or can this be provided? Is the site accessible by public transport from all the areas it is expected to serve? Is pedestrian entry satisfactory? Is there provision for the safe crossing of roads, especially for children and old people? In large and developed towns and cities it is extremely difficult and usually prohibitive in price to acquire a site which is sufficiently large to include all departments, and place each in an ideal relationship to others. L. H. Sidwell at a conference on *Library Buildings: Design and Fulfilment* discussed the building of Holborn Central Library, now in Camden.[1] He suggested that getting the site in the right place was the all-important factor here, and the librarian should not despair too soon of its apparent limitations, as architectural design can make multi-floors and low ceilings an attractive feature. On the other hand, a site should not be accepted which is already too small to meet current potential needs or those which can be estimated in the foreseeable future. It has been stated that libraries should be planned for fifty years ahead, but this is extremely difficult with the growth rate of urban development in many parts of Britain today. A sensible plan often used is to obtain a site which is larger than that at present required, but which will allow scope for enlargement in the future. Alternatively, if sufficient initial capital can be raised, an entire building may be constructed and leased out until needed.

The planning of a new library may be part of a more extensive plan, a community centre or college, a school, a library and health centre or a new housing estate. Buildings which serve two functions have their own problems and advantages, but in general terms unless the library occupies a site in the natural centre of the entire area it may mainly be used by a particular section of the community instead of by the whole potential.

The chief librarian will prepare a brief of requirements giving as full a picture as possible of what the library is going to contain, and of the work to be carried out in the building; he will indicate the position of departments according to noisy and quiet areas. Wheeler and Githens suggest that all equipment, furniture and relationships between departments should be shown in diagrams before being subject to limitations of site, finance and architectural style.[2] The flow of work should be considered. Is there adequate loading and unloading space so that new books can be received immediately on delivery in the book order department without further handling, and be passed on from there to cataloguing and classification, and out again for distribution?

When there is going to be a mobile library based on the branch, is the garage in a position convenient to the unloading bay for prompt withdrawal and replacement of stock? How are the books to reach different departments in the building if they are to be handed in at a centralized desk? Are all departments on the same floor without steps? Will any doors open automatically when approached as in supermarkets or has the member of staff to struggle to open them while pushing a trolley? A book hoist to another floor will require loading and unloading. Is it possible for a lift to be installed for small trolleys of returned books? Some readers may not be able to manage stairs. Are lifts supplied for them? The building should be designed without steps to allow easy access into all public departments by the disabled. The architect may be appointed after winning an architectural competition for the development of a large project; he may be especially commissioned; or the brief may go to the local authority's own architectural department. Once an architect is appointed, co-operation is essential between the architect and the chief librarian and his staff. The librarian and architect may visit different types of new buildings and discuss how problems to do with the site, construction and furnishing were solved, and how problems which were not anticipated have arisen. The external architecture will be planned to blend in with existing buildings of architectural merit, or the library may be a feature in a combined project of several buildings in a civic centre or a shopping plaza. It must be remembered that it will also be subject to the Town and Country Planning Act.

By pleasing design the library should attract readers into it. Formal buildings often look forbidding, particularly to children and young people, but if they can see from outside an informal layout with modern furnishings, and people using the library, they too may be enticed inside. Today, library planning for larger buildings tends to group service departments according to those requiring quiet, fairly noisy, or noisy areas. A children's room should be as far away as possible from a reference library as the level of noise acceptable from children in the library during a busy period is very disturbing to adults who are studying. Ideally a children's library should be on the same floor and reasonably close to the adult library, and if it is to be housed in a separate room children and adults should have free access to each other's library. Browsing areas in the adult library are best planned away from the children's room or section, areas of general circulation or exhibition foyers are more satisfactory in close proximity. Separate entrances from a side road are sometimes provided for children either for reasons of safety or of convenience when classes of children from schools are received. An additional entrance is desirable if the children's library is to be used for lectures, films, and other activities.

Charging of books may take place in the children's room and the advantages of this are that the staff know the children and can discuss any problems of overdue or missing books and keep an eye on the condition in which books are returned. The disadvantages are that a family's books cannot all be exchanged at once and unless there is an assistant to deal with the mechanics of charging at brisk periods the librarian will be too busy to help the children select their books. When there is a centralized counter it should be in the entrance foyer.

It may not be possible to accommodate children's services on the same floor as lending services for adults. In cities or large towns the price of a site may be so expensive or difficult to find that it may be necessary to provide accommodation for children on a higher floor or in a basement. R. Myller in *The Design of the Small Public Library* lists the advantages and disadvantages of mezzanines and basements. As children are generally more energetic than adults they should be the ones to go up or down. Myller also discusses the adaptability of a basement. If the site slopes backwards large windows are possible, but if the land is flat there is a general lack of light, and high windows will be required.[3] Basements tend to be depressing places – of all departments at Holborn Library, Camden, the children's library, which is in a basement, appears the least successful, although a feature has been made of it and it has a magnificent aquarium and a little activities room with a stage. Particular care should be taken that the stairs are safe and not slippery and hand rails should be provided. To cut down noise the stairs may be carpeted. An attractive modern example of a children's library on a mezzanine floor is Burnt Oak Library, Barnet, and a good example of how an older building can be modernized is West Bridgford, Nottinghamshire County, where a reasonable selection of children's books is also available in the main circulating area so that a busy or tired mother does not have to go upstairs to choose books for her children.

Children are frequently catered for as an integral part of the main library which holds a children's book stock of between 1,000 to 7,000 books depending on the size of the child population and use. The deputy branch librarian is sometimes a trained children's librarian and has special responsibility for work with children. How successful this is depends to a large extent on the enthusiasm and interest of the branch librarian concerned, unless a system is in operation where the librarian spends a given amount of time on children's work. In other cases the librarian is appointed as a children's librarian but is in charge of the branch in the absence of the branch librarian.

The advantages of such an open-plan arrangement are that there are no artificial barriers between adults' and children's books, and a large range of stock is displayed for the use of all. Young people will be aware of the layout of the library, and will already know the staff and ask for help. Staff are used to dealing with the whole range of the community which they serve, so there is little chance of them considering themselves solely adult, children's, or reference librarians. There is a danger of this today, particularly in our larger libraries where a direct-entrant, library school graduate could conceivably work in a specialized department for his entire career. A children's librarian must read books intended for adults as well as those published especially for children; she will also need a basic knowledge of reference materials. She must also consider the service as a whole if she is to be a balanced and useful member of the senior staff. The only real disadvantages in an integrated building is that there is considerable difficulty with the reception of school classes and with special activities like lectures or story hours, unless there is a separate activities room, or part of the library which can be partitioned off without preventing other readers from reaching the stock. A few libraries receive the occasional class on a half-day before opening or very early in the morning when there is less inconvenience to other readers. As long as the service in a combined library is essentially a personal one, to all readers, and the staff are not too busy to recognize a child requiring help, the community may be better served. The members of a family may come in together and be near each other while they choose their books. Adults may join the library as a result of coming with their children, or through their own membership become aware of facilities for children. A gay, carefully selected selection of books is a far more compelling advertisement than printed handouts on the services the library offers. Very busy libraries where service at peak periods tends to be impersonal require either a librarian or a trained assistant in the children's section to give help, or a separate children's room. Where there is only one enquiry desk, it should be close to the children's area.

Cities have to decide whether to include facilities for children in libraries which may be some distance from the majority of homes and across dangerous roads, or whether to establish separate children's libraries as was the practice in some boroughs of Central London. Ideally visits to the library should be a family outing, children and parents coming together to select books and records for everyone. If the children's library is separate they are deprived of this joint pleasure. At a talk I gave to a Mothers' Club, one mother said she borrowed books regularly for her children but found it impossible to have books herself unless she saw something she fancied in the older readers' section in the children's library. With a baby and two children under five, she found it impracticable in the adult library to watch them and relax sufficiently to select her own books. Perhaps libraries should consider operating a crèche so that mothers could choose their books in peace. In many areas, for example, the Women's Voluntary Service runs such a crèche, particularly in clinics where mothers attend classes in subjects ranging from child psychology to sewing.

Children's libraries, especially when situated on a large housing estate, tend to become associated with a particular neighbourhood and other children are sometimes reluctant to go there either because they feel they do not belong or, in some cases, because their parents refuse permission. There may be a discipline problem as these libraries tend to get used as a playground and it is very difficult to persuade the children to go to play centres, or the older ones to youth clubs. The problem with older children is never so acute when adult facilities are available or where the library is open plan, as there are books to interest them, and troublemakers are aware that further assistance may be summoned immediately.

The most serious drawback to separate libraries for children is that there cannot be a natural progression to adult stock growing over a period. So there is a sudden severance of the trust that has been built up over the years, right through a child's primary school life, that the library will supply books to meet his recreational and educational needs. He may have been used to visiting the library with his school or have come in after school or on Saturday from a nearby flat, but when the child is moved to a secondary school the nearest adult library may be some distance away. It is unfamiliar and appears very large. He has considerable difficulty in finding his books and is reluctant to ask the staff for help because they all look very busy, and he may not want anything specific but would like to talk about books he may enjoy. This type of relationship is commonplace in the children's library but is more difficult in a busy adult department, although it should continue if there is a librarian on the school premises. Service to adolescents will be more fully covered in chapter 10. Even with a separate children's room, the young person will at least know the children's librarian, who will still be pleased to see him and he will have the opportunity to borrow books from both departments. The librarian will either be able to help him herself in the adult room or introduce him to someone who can. Children's requests cannot always be solved by children's books – a child may want books on antique silver, or on foreign historical coins. An enthusiast will soon have read all the books in the children's library. If it is away from the adult library either the librarian must select a suitable book for him or the child must make a special trip to the adult library. Children's interest is immediate and a book reserved will frequently not be collected, with the exception of books on their own hobbies.

Staffing a children's library in a building on its own is difficult. If it is run as a satellite branch from the nearest district library and different people are sent there, the children lose stability and confidence from not having their own librarian, continuity of the service is jeopardized and staff time is wasted in travelling. On the other hand it may be impossible to justify more than one full-time librarian with the additional services of an assistant and porter during busy periods. Loneliness can become a very real problem especially as social contact with colleagues is an enjoyable feature of work. A librarian appointed to this type of branch needs to have a mature, well-balanced and outgoing personality. She needs to go out into her community to see where she and the library can be of assistance and build up professional and social relationships with others working there in varying fields. As she is in charge of a building, whether or not it is under the indirect charge of the district librarian concerned, her salary should be above that of a children's librarian in a branch. A separate children's library is also extremely expensive. First it must either be built or

2

rented. Where there is also a children's service in a library within reasonable walking distance stock must be purchased for both buildings and also they must both be staffed, heated, lit and maintained.

The City Librarian of Birmingham, in an article in *Library World*, 1967, discussed the dilemma which faces library authorities in how best to provide a library service for children in busy cities.[4] There is of course no ideal solution; he suggested perhaps providing libraries semi-independent of school buildings in the comprehensive schools. There is an interesting example of this at Hazlewick School, Crawley, West Sussex. The library is an attractive hexagonal building separate from the school but connected to it by a covered passageway, and it can also be entered from outside. It gives an immediate appearance of spaciousness and light, and is attractively furnished. It is the school library during the day and a children's library in the evenings, on Saturday mornings and during the holidays. It has one librarian who is both the school and the children's librarian and who buys a stock for both services. As it is situated on a campus it is said that it is not well used during the dark evenings, but neither are many children's libraries in towns.

Leicestershire at present has school libraries which are also public libraries giving service to both adults and children. The schools have the advantage of a large room with both their own stock and that of the county library. From a brief visit to two of these libraries, one at the Ivanhoe Community College, Ashby-de-la-Zouch, and the Hind Leys High School, Stepsted, it appeared that because of lack of space, the schools were relying heavily on the stock of the county and not purchasing sufficient books out of their own capitation grant. One library was also used as a classroom, which meant it would be particularly difficult to entertain classes from other schools, or indeed for other groups of children in the school who might require to use it for reference purposes to go freely into it. There was also a division of authority; the schools had their own teacher librarian, and the county branch was under the control of the group librarian. Stock included school stock, a loan collection from the county library and the branches' own stock. The problem of combined buildings for the ordinary readers as opposed to the schoolchildren, is that schools are not usually situated in the centre of a town. They need plenty of space for gymnasiums, laboratories, playing fields and perhaps a swimming pool, so they are usually situated some distance from the centre. Adults, particularly old people and mothers with young children, may find the library too far away especially if they live on the other side of the town. The hours are limited; it may be impossible to use it during school hours. Mothers find it difficult to bring their young children, especially if they have to meet older ones from school. The problem is particularly difficult for older people in the winter, who like to go out for walks and attend the library in daylight. Leicestershire has varied hours in its schools and community colleges, including Saturdays, to endeavour to come to the best compromise for each community. Cambridgeshire was a pioneer of this type of co-operation with its village colleges and Berkshire has put a public library on a campus where there are several schools.

Trailer libraries may be used to reach communities until a branch is erected, or in places where there are not enough people to justify a library or where there are perhaps perilous roads which cut off a community from the library. The trailer has permanent sites with electrical power and may stay for a few hours or even for a day. The advantages are that the library has a centralized stock instead of scattering it into smaller collections; it is cheaper than renting and maintaining part-time buildings and the public can have the services of a qualified librarian. The disadvantage is that the library is only available at certain stated periods. In Canada bookmobiles frequently carry large children's stocks and in Northern Ontario where a fair proportion of the population are French-speaking, stock must be held in both languages. Crawley places children's books in the schools to be borrowed by the children for home reading instead of carrying them on the trailer.

Camden have satisfied the need for a library with a temporary Terrapin-Reska prefabricated building which has the advantage of very quick assembly. The entire building is tastefully furnished by this firm, and is an extremely inviting example of an integrated adult and junior library with free movement to any section.

Heating and ventilation are extremely important considerations in the design of libraries. The temperature in our buildings should usually be about 68° Fahrenheit, for working in comfort. Methods of central heating include use of gas, electricity, solid fuel, or steam on a district scheme. Underfloor heating has the advantage in children's libraries of providing a warmer floor for younger children to sit on, but carpets cannot be used, which is a decided disadvantage. Other forms of heating include night-storage systems, and heated ceiling panels. It is important in children's libraries to see that any radiators are so placed that they are not too accessible to younger children. Double glazing helps to prevent heat loss, wood is an excellent insulator, but bricks, stone and concrete poor.

Adequate ventilation is also particularly important in a children's library where there may be a lot of people in a relatively small space at one time. Extractor fans may be fitted in roofs with inlets at floor level or through walls, but in industrial areas dirty air is taken in. Downward circulation of air which is purified is usually used with full air-conditioning. When windows can be opened the safety of children must be considered. They should not be able to reach or unfasten any window where there is a drop outside, nor should the windows be so low that a child could fall through them. Care must also be taken with positioning of window seats so that children do not use them to climb up on to the window sill.

It is also necessary to consider both artificial and natural light. The British Lighting Council has recommended fifteen lumens for close work and seven in areas of intermittent reading.[5] It is also important to avoid glare. Sun blinds are useful here and they keep the temperature inside down on a hot, sunny day. Anthony Thompson in *Library Buildings of Britain and Europe* recommends fluorescent lights in libraries, particularly with the use of louvres and reflectors, as there is a larger area of distribution than with filament lights, less risk of glare, and they are closer in colour to natural light and more economical to run.[6] Filament lights need suitable shading or a number of low wattage lamps to prevent glare. Thus study and staff areas will require particular attention, but light must also be carefully diffused and reflected on to the bookshelves. The lighting in West Norwood Library, Lambeth, is an excellent example of careful planning in this field. Stairs must be well lit so that all steps can be clearly seen, and when there is a side entrance that is not on a well-lit street adequate lighting should be provided at the entrance. Interior decoration will also reflect light – a ceiling between 80 and 85 per cent, walls 50–60 per cent. This must be borne in mind when redecorating. Very light colours will increase the amount of light in the room but can also cause glare, particularly when the surface is shiny. This also applies to furniture which has a light reflection of between 35 and 50 per cent and floors between 15 and 30 per cent.

Floor covering may vary in different parts of the library according to the degree of use and quiet required. Covering must be considered for durability, maintenance, non-slip qualities, warmth, noise, design, variety and cost. Thompson has a table listing varying surfaces and assessing them from these points of view. Parquet and hard-wood block flooring is expensive to install, needs treatment to be non-slip, tends to get damaged by heels and is noisy but it is extremely attractive when well maintained. Linoleum is cheap, non-slip, and in a variety of colours, but is harder to maintain than plastic tiles, like those made from PVC and thermoplastics which are available in many colours, but which require sealing when first laid and need special polishing. Heavy-wear carpet gives a more informal appearance, is warm, non-slip, muffles sound and can stand up surprisingly well to heavy use. Carpet tiles are also practical as they can be replaced as required. The floor covering will also be determined by the type of heating which has been installed.

Libraries should be planned into quiet and noisy areas. Thompson suggests fifty phons as the accepted level of noise in lending departments, but children's libraries may well be higher. Acoustic panels in the ceiling, wall shelving and books, and carpeting, or cork floor covering, will help to muffle internal noise. Chairs should be fitted with ferrules if on a hard floor to minimize noise and prevent scuffing. Any noise from outside which can be heard inside the library building must also be considered, and double glazing and insulation can help to deaden it.

REFERENCES

1 Library Association. London and Home Counties Branch. *Library Buildings: Design and Fulfilment*. London, Library Association, 1967.
2 J. L. Wheeler and A. M. Githens. *The American Public Library Building*. New York, Scribner, 1941.
3 R. Myller. *The Design of the Small Public Library*. New York, Bowker, 1966.
4 W. A. Taylor. 'Library Work with Children in a Large City'. *Library World*, vol. 68, no. 803, May 1967. pp. 295–301.
5 British Lighting Council. *Interior Lighting Design Handbook*. London, British Lighting Council, 1965.
6 Anthony Thompson. *Library Buildings of Britain and Europe*. London, Butterworths, 1963.

FURTHER READING

Berriman, S. G. *Library Buildings 1967–1968*. London, Library Association, 1969.
Berriman, S. G. and K. C. Harrison. *British Public Library Buildings*. Grafton. London, André Deutsch, 1966.
Stockham, K. A. 'Branch Library Buildings'. *Proceedings of the Public Libraries Conference Held at Dublin, 1967*. London, Library Association, 1967. pp. 7–12.

Chapter 3
Interior Décor

The interior of a library should be planned to give readers easy access to all facilities offered. The décor should be relaxing, comfortable and contemporary (but not ultra-modern in an older building) to encourage readers to linger if they have time.

Children's libraries and areas should be informal and inviting. As they cater for all ages, from toddlers to those at secondary school, care must be taken that while suitable provisions are made for little children, the section does not resemble a kindergarten. The library may be open plan and a part of the lending library. It may be screened off with glass screens as in the Manor Branch, Sheffield, or it may have a temporary screen sliding into a wall, enabling it to be shut off if an activity is being held in the room, as at Church Street District Library, Westminster. A building should be designed to be flexible internally so that departments may be moved, enlarged or made smaller to meet future needs. Modular planning based on load-supporting columns at a standard distance apart – Manor Branch is a 13ft. 6in. × 13ft. 6in. module – makes removal of internal screens or furniture to change the position of departments or storage areas a simple matter. Without structural walls rooms can be easily enlarged and layout altered.

Lionel McColvin in *Public Library Services for Children* suggested suites of rooms for children.[1] They could solve the problem of dealing with a wide age range and allow other activities to take place without disturbing children who come in to change books. Even in a large room without internal division, children tend to group themselves in particular areas and they move seats to whichever area they are occupying. Free-standing shelving and display screens can be made to form attractive alcoves where tables and chairs and the younger children's sections can be grouped. The bays should not be more than 3ft. 6in. high both for appearance and supervision. If suites of rooms are planned there must be adequate staff to supervise them, or the children's librarian's desk must be strategically placed allowing immediate accessibility and visibility to all parts. Adequate workroom space is also essential close to the library.

With the tendency towards smaller houses and flats and with children living in twilight areas in cities, it is important that consideration should be given to where children are going to do their homework. On a busy evening to study in a children's library can be disturbing. Several authorities provide study areas with suitable reference books. Many libraries will allow children to use the reference library but in a town with many students and space at a premium this may be impossible. It is a nuisance when books from the children's library have to be moved to the reference library because other readers may need to refer to the books.

Many children's libraries have been planned so that they can double for a meeting or activities room. It is unfortunate to have to close the children's library whenever an activity is taking place particularly if it is intended to stimulate interest in books and reading. If there is not a lecture or activities room it should be possible to screen off an area so that the majority of the books are available for loan or consultation. Bright-coloured curtains can become an attractive feature of a room as at Coalville, Leicestershire, where part of the upper floor is used for children's activities. Book talks and story hours can be held conveniently when an area is an integral part of the children's library. Modern Canadian libraries often have beautiful story areas like Jones Children's Library, a branch of Toronto Public Libraries, and Etobicoke Central Library which is in a well, and is brought immediately to the newcomer's attention by a brilliant crimson carpet. Luton has a story room which opens through a mural panelled door. It is designed like a fairy castle, the ceiling a night sky with lights as stars.

In cities today when so many mothers are working, children are left to their own devices during the school holidays. In parts of Central London, and this is probably common in many cities, there appear to be too few outdoor play areas in the summer, and in the winter when the weather is bad there are few places to go in the holidays other than the library. Many children are in the library day in and day out and require more strenuous activity. Some libraries organize story hours, story and painting sessions, model-making, drama clubs, masks and puppetry, and a room where these activities could be carried out would be invaluable.

All libraries should include public lavatories and if it proves necessary the doors can be locked and opened when required. Crawley has included a wash-basin in a semi-private part of the children's library as many of the children travel some distance and cannot go home quickly to wash their hands if necessary. As long as the child is not made to feel embarrassed this type of facility is a good idea.

Cloakrooms where coats and hats may be hung in wet or cold weather are an excellent feature, but unless they are attended they should be inside the children's library as at Churchill Gardens, Westminster. This library also has a beautiful little courtyard with troughs of flowers and plants – glass doors open out on it from the library. Lambeth's West Norwood branch also has a large courtyard in the centre of the library with plenty of all-weather chairs where readers may sit on fine days. These courtyards give an appearance of spaciousness and it is possible to forget one is in the centre of a town or city; they are a much better idea than placing a library in a park.

The International Federation of Library Associations Standards,[2] which agree with the recommendations of the Library Association,[3] suggest 50 sq.ft. for the children's department for every 1,000 population, with the proviso that it should be large enough to accommodate a school class. They also state that in large urban areas children should not have to travel far to the library. It is unlikely that a children's library would have to serve a population of over 30,000, so 1,500 sq.ft. is usually sufficient.

The furnishing of the children's section or room will be in keeping with the rest of the library. In modern buildings with large glass windows, which are an excellent advertisement from the outside, there may be little wall space to fix wall shelving and many of the shelves will have to be free standing.

The Library Association Standards recommend that there should be 190 children's books on open shelves for every 1,000 population served. The Bourdillion Report[4] stated that provision of children's books cannot be directly related to population but that a library providing a basic service should purchase a minimum of 1,500 books of which half would be replacements and duplicates. IFLA standards suggest that in a medium-sized library approximately twenty per cent of the shelf space should be in the children's department. Thus if we take the Library Association standards as a guide, a town or branch library serving a population of 30,000 would require 5,700 books on the open shelves in an area of 1,500 sq. ft. The Bourdillion working party's comment on the IFLA standards suggested that 4,000–6,000 volumes should be the optimum shelf capacity, as there is a limited number of worthwhile children's books.

Shelving which is architect-designed for a specific building is usually expensive, but then it suits the characteristics of a particular building and avoids standardization in appearance of different libraries. It is costly to add to later. Bays are frequently 3ft. wide but these can be adjusted to fit in with the dimensions of the room. Notes of any variations should be carefully filed in the library concerned and in the administrative office in case new guiding is being ordered in later years which involves fixing anything across the fascia of the shelves, like metal strips in magnetic guiding. Wood shelving is still very popular in British libraries and homes. The natural grain is attractive to the eye and wood is less harsh and much warmer than metal. As a frame it displays books well, and other furniture can be ordered in a similar finish. Light oak, dark oak, sapele and mahogany finish are commonly used. When ordering additional items the type of finish should be stated and if possible a specimen enclosed. Metal shelving is available in attractive designs and shades from a variety of firms.

Wall shelving may be either fitted directly to the wall by using uprights like Spur, or metal rod ladders like Scott Smith. Reska have an extremely versatile unit which incorporates picture book boxes, which all make the floor appear less crowded and make cleaning easy. Reska, Spur and Versatile Fittings have excellent book supports which are easily adjusted, and also back supports which can be altered as required. Libraco, Librex and Remploy supply more traditional-looking shelving.

The height of wall shelving for children should be a maximum of 5ft. 6in. including fascia, allowing four shelves to each stack including the bottom shelf and a minimum of 11in. between shelves. Five shelves can be accommodated in some sections but if space is not at a premium fewer are more attractive. As adults are consulting and straightening the books a plinth of at least 9in. is desirable at the base, and 9in. depth except for oversize and young children's books. Adjustable shelving is essential and will include tonks fittings, slots or ladders to hold the shelf in position. Low shelving, as at Swiss Cottage, Camden, is an extremely attractive feature, but many of the children's staff and adults will have to stoop. Free-standing shelving must be lower or it will spoil the appearance of the room and make supervision more difficult. A height of 3ft 6in. is applicable, on double-sided shelving; this will give three shelves on each side and 4–5ft. for wall shelving. Adult libraries estimate 10 books per foot of shelving but in children's libraries this is far too few. A recent check averaged 15 books per foot in the fiction section, and 23 in the non-fiction section. Reference books are approximately 8 per foot, while over-size are 8–12 per foot. Shelves should be adjustable but allow for 12-in. depth and 15in. between shelves in both sections. Shelves which may be used either flat or sloping like Reska or Scott Smith are useful for displaying books, and making the shelves appear reasonably full, especially in a new library when demand has been particularly heavy.

For little children, the 'Kinderbox' is very popular. If a box of this type is to be bought or made the divisions should not be more than 7in. in depth or small children will have difficulty in getting books out of them, and they must be adequately divided internally or the books become very untidy. Nottinghamshire County use display boards with their groups of boxes and the 'Kinderpit' at West Norwood has an ingeniously attractive seating arrangement for small children incorporating four 'Kinderboxes' at the corners. A run of special shelving can also be made with bins for large picture books. It is necessary to have thin dividers approximately every 6in. Younger children's shelving should not be more than 3ft. high, but 1ft. deep and include display racks. Adjustable back rests and mobile book-rests, which hold the books upright, are invaluable in this section where runs of extremely large and tiny books have to be accommodated close together. East York Library near Toronto has a large unit designed with long, narrow pigeon-holes holding about six large picture books each, and a run of smaller ones above this for the oblong-shaped books and small books. Young children can easily reach the book required without knocking a row down. Above this is a display rack for picture books, but little children require help in reaching them.

It may also be necessary to clear the floor for library activities. If there are free-standing cases on the floor, wheels and brakes will be essential. It would be useful if a 'Kinderbox' could be supplied which is mobile when required, but with a safe-breaking device, as they are extremely heavy to move when laden.

Guiding is more satisfactory if broad headings are given either on the tops of shelving, or with island shelving, on the side of the tiers if these and not the shelves are visible when entering the room. Specific subject numbers will be shown in the subject index. If the layout of the library is not obvious when entering the room, a simple plan in the children's library or a duplicated one is useful. Staff should do everything possible to show a new member round the library.

The type of guiding chosen should be flexible, but not removable by children. The pin type of individual letters which may be stuck into cork is extremely adjustable, but children are tempted to form them into rude words, and they can be dangerous if they become loose and fall off. Shelves may also be made with a groove, so that guiding may be inserted. Letraset which is available in varying colours, sizes and typeface is useful here. Different-coloured backgrounds can denote fiction and non-fiction but the guiding must be easily visible in natural and artificial light. Library suppliers make up guiding to the clients' own specifications which may be screwed in to the tops of shelves. Magnetic guiding is extremely versatile; a strip of metal is placed on the top of the shelves. As with other guiding it is made up in colour, type-face, size and phrases required, and there is a magnet on the back which attaches itself to a metal strip.

Colour may be introduced into the library by formica-topped tables, and coloured, upholstered chairs. Tables may be obtained from many retail firms or contract suppliers and may have metal or wooden frames and should be chosen to blend in with shelving and other furnishings of a library. In a new building all furniture may come from one supplier; Cheam Branch of Sutton is furnished by Scott Smith, and Luton by Conran. Tables are available in a variety of shapes – round, square, oblong. Formica is more practical than wood if children are going to paint, crayon or use ink for their homework. It is available in a variety of colours and patterns. Tables of different colour and sizes may be attractively grouped together and can always be separated if more seating is required. When there is not a study room or area, children will have to work in the children's library but it is important not to lose the spacious appearance of the room. It is better perhaps to provide table space for a maximum of sixteen children initially and if there is room and it is necessary, buy more later. Children who are reading but not writing or consulting several books can be accommodated on bench window seats. School libraries would expect to accommodate more, and libraries might be badly placed if a class of forty came to work on a project. Buckingham Palace Road Library in Westminster found old collapsible tables, which had been replaced in another branch, very useful in this situation. An occasional low coffee table with low armchairs encourage adults and older children to browse, and give the library an informal appearance.

Chairs should not be purchased from a catalogue; they must be sat on for a few minutes and compared for comfort. Chairs which do not support the back are particularly uncomfortable for sitting on for long periods. Upholstered chairs are usually more comfortable than wooden ones, but they must be in a spongeable material, or if of fabric they must be zipped or tied so that they can easily be removed for regular cleaning. Window bench seating is always popular with children, and there are informal free-standing benches which will seat two large children comfortably. The colourful couches at the Swiss Cottage Library, Camden, are an excellent feature. Stacking chairs must be checked to see that they do in fact stack. Some advertised as such are unsatisfactory, especially as regards weight. The linking device should also be effective.

Little children are not very comfortable with their legs dangling from chairs, and small tables and chairs will be disconcerting to older children. Stools with legs which have to screw into the seat can be dangerous if they become loose. Large pouffes can be purchased in bright colours and spongeable materials from retail stores. It is well worth carpeting the younger children's area if not the entire library so that small children may sit or lie on their tummies to look at books. Carpets have stood up to extremely hard wear in two of Central London's libraries and in one case where there is also a wood-block floor, the carpet is in much better condition and requires far less maintenance. Carpet tiles are also available and are easily replaced if damaged. A slope for picture books with a low bench seat are useful for young children who will have difficulty in turning the pages of a book while holding it. The slope may be double-sided if desired, and a coloured formica slope on a wooden frame gives an attractive background to the books. Cushions or hassocks are a good idea for story time or short book talks for children of primary school age, and can be easily moved. It is essential that they are of good quality; cheap garden cushions do not stand up to this type of wear. The interiors should be made of such a substance as Dunlopillo, or one piece of latex, or feather (if the latter there must be an inner and outer covering), and the exterior should be spongeable, or if of fabric be zippable for washing or dry-cleaning. Retail stores may arrange a contract order at a reduced price.

Curtains can soften the appearance of a rather austere room, apart from the obvious advantage of enabling a room to be blacked out for varying activities. Lined curtains hang better and suffer less damage from the sun, and material is now available already lined. It is the soft furnishings in exquisite colours which make Swiss Cottage Library, Camden, so pleasing to the eye.

Periodical racks and stands for paperbacks will also be required. They may be designed especially for the library concerned, but lightweight enamelled wire ones may be bought from library suppliers.

If records are available, and are on open access, a browser box will be necessary which will include sections for 7in. and 12in. records, and have room for sets such as Junior Linguaphone.

Storage of filmstrips, films, audio- and video-tapes will have to be given thoughtful attention in public libraries as well as in schools and separate resource centres. As information is not necessarily in print, and more equipment is in domestic use, borrowing facilities will be required for many types of materials.

A short course was organized by the Youth Libraries Group in 1972 in which students had the opportunity of visiting resource centres in the London area and discussing the problems of establishing them.

With the advent of the computer catalogue cabinets may well become as outdated as the indicator did after the introduction of open access. Cabinets are available from library suppliers in modern and traditional design for use with 5in. × 3in. catalogue cards. The design appears to influence the capacity, so care must be taken that sufficient drawers are purchased initially. It is advisable to inform the firm concerned, if the cabinet is to be freestanding, that it is intended for a children's library and that it is essential that it should be steady. Rods are necessary; in theory a rod opened from the back is safer but it is a nuisance to have to take the drawer out to reach the rod.

Children tend to use the subject index more than the catalogue, and the visible subject index is popular. Panels may be obtained with stands or fixed to a suitable surface. As long as a panel is not allowed to become too full, typed headings on strips may be inserted easily.

When charging takes place in the children's library a counter will be required. The type of counter will depend on the issue scheme in use, as more space will be required for Browne than Token or Photocharging. Where readers' tickets and bookcards are filed in order as in Browne, the issue should be sunken into the desk so it does not get knocked off accidentally. In busy libraries there should be separate places for books to be marked out and discharged, with a flat surface for children to place books when returning them. Space will also be necessary for reserved books, books needing repair or withdrawal, the file of registered readers, tickets not in use, and all types of stationery. The counter should not be more than 3ft. in height, so that small children can be seen – staff should sit down – and it should not be so large that it forms a barrier. A library supplier will adapt a standard unit or units to specifications which is cheaper, although it may be less attractive, than an architect-designed one made entirely to specification by craftsmen. When charging is centralized the librarian will need more space in her own desk for stationery, and possibly drawers adapted to take the readers' voucher file if she is going to register new readers, and shelves included in her desk or behind it for reserved books if she is handing them out. Again standard units can be adapted for this.

Insufficient attention is paid to display when planning the interiors of new children's rooms. A glass display case properly lit is good for valuable articles such as manuscripts, original illustrations, pottery and coins, but children love to see and handle their own work displayed in the library. Schools do imaginative art work, which they are usually pleased to lend or give to the library for display. Wall space above bookshelves, particularly those for younger children, is excellent for a display area of cork or hessian. An occasional cork or hessian panel is useful in a row of bookshelves as long as the displays or posters are attractive. There is no excuse for scrappy handwritten notices today: letraset and display type-faces can ensure a neat appearance. Additional display equipment which is mobile and collapsible is required for special exhibitions of books, models and posters. Marler Haley have particularly versatile display equipment which is easily assembled. County libraries set up a considerable number of exhibitions outside the libraries, especially for teachers. Nottinghamshire County appear to have paid particular attention to display in the planning of their libraries. Lambeth have put on excellent exhibitions of foreign books and Swiss Cottage Library's display area, which is centrally placed for all departments, has some excellent equipment, and some exhibitions have been put on there to appeal to all age groups.

Libraries are required to submit estimates for the following financial year several months before it begins in April. Before planning for additional items in the estimates, the whole décor and proportion of the room must be considered, and whether or not any additions will enhance the interior design or detract from it.

REFERENCES

1 Lionel R. McColvin. *Public Library Services for Children*. Paris, UNESCO, 1957.
2 International Federation of Library Associations. *Standards of Public Library Service – Library Premises*. (Memorandum approved in principle at Warsaw, 1959.) Extracts and working party comments in Appendix 3, the Bourdillion Report (see note 4 below).
3 Library Association. *Public Library Buildings: the Way Ahead*, 1960. Extracts and working party comments in Appendix 3, the Bourdillion Report (see note 4 below).
4 Ministry of Education. *Standards of Public Library Service in England and Wales. Report of the Working Party Appointed by the Ministry of Education in March 1961* (Bourdillion Report). London, HMSO, 1962.

Chapter 4
Duties of the Children's Librarian

A librarian is responsible for making readily available, and maintaining, a collection of books or other materials to serve the needs of his readers. The clientèle in the library varies; it may be entirely for students in a college, or a business firm, or it may be one of several departments in a public library catering especially for music, reference and study, housebound readers or children. The Roberts Report, 1959[1] and the Bourdillion Report, 1962[2] stressed the need for attracting and retaining more specialist librarians by improving their salaries and career prospects. Today, especially, when direct entrants from schools of librarianship may work immediately in specialized departments, it is essential that they are aware of the facilities offered by other departments and libraries. We may be able to departmentalize our stock and staff, but our readers and their interests will never fall into neat compartments.

The children's librarian must be a part of the community in which she works. She should be in close liaison with other organizations which cater for children and young people: teachers, health visitors, nursery nurses, playgroup leaders, probation officers, youth officers, local organizations for mentally- or physically-handicapped children, gifted children, play leaders and the Council of Social Service, which may organize play centres in the holidays and have an overseas committee to help immigrants integrate into the community. She should also read council meeting and committee minutes and local newspapers which give an idea of future developments, particularly housing, health and education and welfare. To know where the children live, where they play, and which roads are difficult to cross is all part of the work, enabling one to be *en rapport* in conversations with children, their parents and teachers.

The children's librarian is especially concerned with building up a good collection of books and other materials which will be of interest to children, and to their parents and other adults working with them or for them, such as teachers, authors, illustrators and publishers. She may be in charge of a service for children in both public libraries and schools, in libraries only, with the Education Department running the school service as in the Inner London Educational Authority, or she may be a branch children's librarian responsible for work with children in the library, or a regional children's librarian responsible for a group of libraries. Her mind must be alert and she should be receptive to new ideas and able to evaluate them. Finally she must be in contact with other librarians doing similar or related work so that there is co-operation and exchange of ideas.

To work with children in a library is enjoyable and extremely rewarding, but it is essential to like children without being sentimental about them, to be patient and never to force assistance but to show them you are there to help if they want you. Sometimes, as even adult readers do, they find it difficult to explain what they really want, and it is important to be careful to question them gently. It is also necessary to be a good listener; children need you as a friend and want to tell you about events in their everyday life which are important to them. However, at the same time you must keep an unobtrusive eye open for the child who may require help but is too shy to ask.

A children's library should have a relaxed and happy atmosphere and quiet conversation should be encouraged. Reasonable discipline is essential and determination is necessary in dealing with unruly children who should not be allowed to spoil the library for everyone else. A gentle reminder usually suffices for an unintentional or thoughtless incident, but if there is a definite attempt to undermine authority or extreme rudeness, the child or children should be warned that, if they continue to behave in this way, they will have to leave the library for the day and the librarian should be prepared to carry out any threat made. Holidays are a particular problem, now that so many mothers work. The children become bored, especially when there are not any indoor play centres. They gravitate towards the library because it is warm, comfortable and free and they have nowhere else to go. Berwick Sayers in *A Manual of Children's Libraries* suggested that staff working in children's libraries should have shorter hours than other staff as the strain is greater.[3]

The selection, withdrawal, maintenance and revision of stock is of paramount importance. The senior children's librarian is usually given a total book fund and is responsible for allocation to all service-points. A stated sum of money may be given to each branch, which involves considerable clerical work, or it may be based on the average price of a book the system buys, allowing for an increase in price each year. Each library will then purchase a given number of volumes, including new books and replacements and the senior children's librarian will have to check that the value of the unit is realistic and make adjustment if expedient, later in the financial year.

The International Federation of Library Associations suggests that one-fifth of the total stock should be for children.[4] The Library Association[5] figure is 190 children's books for every thousand population and Bourdillion suggests that at least 1,500 children's books should be bought annually by any library providing a basic library service. It was further suggested that in a children's library duplication and replacement was usually not less than 100 per cent, so that would result in 750 new titles per annum, about one-third of the annual publishing output in 1962. Danish standards provide four books for each child from 0–13 resident in the area if the school also loans books for home reading, otherwise six.[6] They also suggest that wear and tear would require one book to be replaced for every forty issues.

The fewer children living in the area the more books *per capita* are essential, and it is extremely expensive to fragment the service especially into part-time children's libraries. Peggy Heeks mentioned a minimum shelf stock of 1,000 books rising to 5,000 in more populous areas.[7] With the lower figure a comprehensive home reading service in the school would be essential as it would be impossible to include both the standard fiction and non-fiction to answer homework enquiries, interests and hobbies, and picture books for younger children. It would also be necessary to have some system of circulating stock between libraries so as to inject sufficient variety.

When allocating the book fund the senior children's librarian will consider the potential users, i.e. those who have not yet started school and those of school age. If the town is one people tend to come to from the surrounding area and also visit the library, this will also have to be taken into account. The shelf capacity must be considered, the number of registered readers, and the number of issues per book in stock. The condition of the stock should be kept at an equal level throughout the system. Apart from hard use, physical conditions in the library and homes may vary greatly even in one city, and the books will need replacing at a different rate.

To return to allocation of the book fund, any new developments in housing, schools or the opening of playgroups will result in heavier use. It may be more economical to provide a special collection of books for a playgroup bulk loan. Westminster sends twenty books to groups, and changes them about every two months. Playgroups prefer a reasonably long loan. Comments are asked for on the books supplied and books may be requested. Where possible it is preferable for the playgroup to come to the library, listen to a story and choose their own books, but often the playgroups are too far away from a children's room or the roads are too dangerous.

The only thoroughly reliable way of choosing books is by reading and reviewing them, preferably by two members of staff if one is inexperienced. Hertfordshire have an extremely comprehensive scheme involving subject specialists. Leicestershire review all books and shortened reviews appear in *Learning Resources* which is sent to schools each term, and this is also an ordering device for the schools purchasing service. Frederick Hallworth also describes school book provision in Wiltshire in the *Library World*, December 1967, which involves local specialists in the reviewing scheme.[8] The possibility of co-operative book selection meetings and reviewing between schools and neighbouring authorities could be explored further in this country. There are some excellent co-operative schemes in the United States between libraries and science faculties.

The librarian must co-relate her book selection policy to that of other departments of the public library and schools. In highly specialized subjects and in the scientific field, librarians may have difficulty in assessing a book. *The School Librarian* reviews are particularly helpful. Other periodicals which are useful for their reviews are *Children's Book Review, Junior*

Bookshelf, the children's book supplements of *The Times Literary Supplement*, *The Times Educational Supplement* and *Growing Point*. Other periodicals and daily and Sunday newspapers review children's books from time to time especially at Christmas, and John Rowe Townsend and Brian Alderson give sterling service to children's literature in the *Guardian* and *The Times*. Some authorities review some of the books which are sent on approval and examine the rest; others examine them but do not review. With an experienced staff this is fairly satisfactory, but sufficient time must be allowed and the odd book is rejected which would have been accepted if read and vice versa. When books are reviewed, staff should be given the opportunity to see the review and examine the book.

The library may make its own arrangement for the supply of approval copies on publication from a library supplier or bookseller. Some libraries prefer the bookseller to do a preliminary sifting out of the less worthwhile material. It may be a policy to purchase all copies sent, or they may be supplied on a sale or return basis, extra copies being marked up on a duplicate copy of the list which is returned to the supplier. Others return all copies and order separately. A file card must be retained giving author, title, publisher, date, edition, bookseller, date ordered, number of copies required and location. A card should be filed for all books rejected. Any reports on delay of supply should be marked and outstanding books for which there is not a report can be chased as necessary. This card may possibly be used in the master catalogue, but this will depend on the audit system.

Children's libraries buy a considerable number of replacements and some libraries produce standard lists of books which should always be in stock. These must, of course, be constantly revised and kept up to date. Particular care should be taken in the replacement of subjects which undergo considerable change and here a visit to a supplier with a comprehensive stock is invaluable. A supplier will send a list of books selected for confirmation so if in doubt it is possible to check stock and reviews before finally committing an order.

Caution must be exercised when withdrawing stock so that valuable out-of-print material is not withdrawn and that consideration is given to books which would be useful in reserve stock. When the library co-operates in a specialization scheme such as the Metropolitan Joint Fiction Reserve anything coming within the library's category should be checked to ensure that it is in stock. Many libraries buy titles in their category as they appear in the British National Bibliography, and they are placed immediately with the adult books in the scheme.

Where there is an efficient local bookshop, the library will normally purchase books from it, but the bookshop's busiest period is before Christmas which is also the time when the library is buying heavily from the new autumn publications. Libraries can help by ordering their replacements during the slack period in the summer, but they may be faced with a storage problem as it is the time of year when shelves become overcrowded. Anne Benson, the School Library Adviser at Sisson and Parker, ably discussed at the Holborn Conference in 1966 the problems of a bookseller serving both the public and school and public libraries; whether or not it was advisable to have two separate stocks, problems of space in a good central position and the small margin of profit especially when libraries required books to be serviced.[9] The difficulties of servicing books for libraries, and lack of standardization was covered in greater detail by W. H. S. Whitehouse of C. Combridge Limited at the same meeting.[10]

On what criteria do we select books for our children's libraries? Unfortunately if library book-buying hits the headlines it is from the negative rather than the positive point of view, and some adults tend to forget that publishing has not come to an abrupt end since they were children. Excellent books are being written by accomplished authors today, and it is a tragedy if through replacing books which once had their heyday, sufficient copies of worthwhile new books are not available to stimulate the imagination of today's children.

When considering any book we must ask ourselves if the author really knows his subject. This applies in fiction as much as in non-fiction. Leon Garfield and Hester Burton have been extremely careful of the historical accuracy in their novels. Veronica Robinson writes very convincingly of the problems of a deaf child in *David in Silence*. In fantasy, is the means of reaching the other place or time imaginative as in *The Night Watchmen* by Helen Cresswell, *Earth Fasts* by William Mayne, and *Elidor* by Alan Garner? It is of primary importance to consider the following: Is it a good story, is the plot well developed, are the characters alive, how do they develop in themselves and in their relationships with each other? The story must be well written and the vocabulary, actions and objects must be in keeping with the period or place in which the story is set. This again comes back to the first point about an author really knowing and being immersed in his subject. Rosemary Sutcliff's historical novels are model examples and *The Dream Time* by Henry Treece is convincing. At the first International Summer School at Loughborough Hester Burton described how she was influenced to write about events in an earlier period by parallels of similar occurrences in her own lifetime, e.g. the similarity of Britain's isolation in the Second World War before America came in and the country's isolation at the time of Trafalgar in *Castors Away*.

In non-fiction, apart from an author knowing his subject does he present it in a way which is comprehensible to children without writing down to them? Is the subject appropriate to the interests of the children of the age group it is written for? Are the diagrams and illustrations clear and informative and is there an index? Finally, how does it compare with other books we already have in stock on this subject? Books which require child participation, such as science experiments, ballet and underwater swimming, should be looked at or reviewed by an expert to see that the practical work is safe. Good non-fiction is often extremely attractively illustrated today. The Bodley Head have published a series on animal life which delight children, by authors of the calibre of Gwynne Vevers, Alfred Leutscher and W. E. Swinton. *The Bayeux Tapestry* was imaginatively reproduced by Norman Denny and Josephine Filmer-Sankey. Walter Hodges has done some beautiful drawings for several books including *Shakespeare's Theatre*, while Alan Sorrell and Ian Ribbons have made an excellent contribution to the history section.

Picture books account for a considerable proportion of the book fund, but they also cover a large age range. I have discussed them more fully in the first chapter and with regard to story-telling in Chapter 8. It is important that children should be exposed to good art from their earliest years, and there are some really excellent picture books available. They are expensive to produce and although the price is kept down by simultaneous publication, they are still costly to buy in sufficient quantity. There are arguments against dressed animals. Lillian H. Smith ably discussed the work of Beatrix Potter in the outstanding criticism of literature for children *The Unreluctant Years*.[11] She attributed the success of these stories to the creation of a miniature world that a little child could comprehend. Animals in the stories retain their own characteristics and the natural enmities prevail.

Books of fairytales, hero stories and legends require care in selection. Frequently re-tellings are in a language so mundane that the magic of the tale is lost, and the plot may be altered. Re-tellers should state the original source used, and comparison of the different versions of the same tale is helpful here. Kathleen Lines, Virginia Haviland, Peggy Appiah and Ruth Manning-Sanders have done excellent work in this field. Some of the single individual fairytales in picture-book format are delightful. Margery Gill, Barry Wilkinson, William Stobbs and Marcia Brown have accepted a challenge to illustrate old tales of which we all have our own mental image.

Poetry is popular with children but more really good anthologies which also look attractive are required. It is impossible to reach saturation point with *The Oxford Book of Poetry*, edited by Edward Blishen and illustrated by Brian Wildsmith, and *The Golden Treasury of Poetry*, edited by Louis Untermeyer.

The extent of the reference stock will depend on local conditions; where the library is a modern open-plan room, incorporating a reference section, there is no point in duplicating material which is readily available. On the other hand where the reference library is extremely busy and study space is oversubscribed as in university towns, a more comprehensive collection will be required in the children's library. A study room is desirable in populous areas where children may do their homework and/or work on school projects; the reference collection can be housed there and also books of information available for loan. When a book is only available for reference its potential use is limited, and duplication of popular material like stamp catalogues in lending and reference stock is desirable.

The most recent copies of encyclopedias will only be available for use in the library. The *Oxford Junior Encyclopaedia* (2nd ed. 1964, 13 vols.), is extremely useful for the 11–19 age group, but the classified arrangement may be explained to younger children; it is now under continuous revision. *Children's Britannica* (2nd ed. 1969, 20 vols.) is factually sound, while *Pears Encyclopaedia* is useful for quick reference and home-lending.

Several companies sell encyclopedias direct to libraries and schools. Representatives produce a mock volume which includes articles from all volumes. Obviously this is a selling device, and an encyclopedia should never be ordered without examining the set. It is good practice as in Leicestershire to circularize schools with an evaluative review of the work. Points to be considered are factual accuracy, clear succinct definitions and description, whether the style and tone of writing, format and illustrations are clear and appropriate to the age group and interests of children for whom it is intended. Is the indexing satisfactory and how current are the articles? The date of publication may be little indication. Articles on the sciences or on the newly developed countries, for example, will show how up-to-date an encyclopedia is. A new edition may be compared with an older edition and with other encyclopedias. An important practical factor is whether individual volumes can be replaced if they are stolen or damaged.

There should be English dictionaries and also English into foreign languages like French and German and vice versa. *The Hamish Hamilton Children's Dictionary* is a straightforward one for young children; *Chambers Children's Illustrated Dictionary* includes pronunciation, parts of speech and illustrated difficult words. *Junior Illustrated Dictionary* by E. L. Thorndike is more useful for older children.

Gazetteers and atlases are important and there should be books which show the political and geological parts of the world. It is essential that they, like the globe, which is a popular and useful reference tool, are up to date.

Standard quick reference works which are frequently used by children include *Whitaker's Almanack, Who's Who* and *The Guinness Book of Records*.

It is important tnat the librarian should show the child how to find information from books and a comprehensive range of study books should be available for home use.

Good reference services for young people may encourage teenagers to use libraries. Walsall has selected part of its stock with the secondary school syllabus in mind. Advice on careers, vertical files of information too recent to be included in books, and periodicals to complement the book stock may all help to provide this service.

Periodicals are popular for browsing in children's libraries. Copies of periodicals of permanent use such as *Animals* and *Pictorial Education* should be bound or retained for an Illustrations Collection. Others such as *Aeromodeller* and *Meccano Magazine* may be held for a specified period and then given to interested children.

The *Junior Bookshelf*, *Children's Book Review*, the *School Librarian* and *Signal*, will be purchased primarily for parents, teachers, and staff. *Puffin Post* and *Elizabethan* include book reviews written for children and teenagers.

Records available for children are gradually becoming part of the stock. Sometimes they are placed in the music library and sometimes in the children's library. Open access in low browser boxes is essential for children and either the entire record or the outer sleeve will be displayed. Polythene inner sleeves will be required and the outer sleeve should be strengthened. There is a reasonable range of material suitable for children including music, poetry, story-telling, bird songs and their recognition, and language records. There is controversy over whether or not to include pop records, but standards should be as high as in book selection and records judged on their individual merit.

Fourteen-inch long-playing records can be expensive, but some of these may be bought if cheaper, but good, recordings like those found in the Decca, Ace of Spades and the EMI Music for Pleasure series are included. Ten-inch records are fairly cheap.

It is essential to have several copies of *Peter and the Wolf* by Sergei Prokofiev and *The Young Person's Guide to the Orchestra* by Benjamin Britten. *Carnival of the Animals* by Saint-Saëns and *Let's Make an Opera* by Benjamin Britten are also popular. Poetry is well catered for in *Poetry and Song* and *Rhyme and Rhythm* recorded by Argo in association with Macmillan; Peter Ustinov reads *Cautionary Verses* and T. S. Eliot his poems in *Old Possum's Book of Practical Cats*.

Story-telling includes Andersen, Grimm and a delightful collection of African stories told by Hugh Tracey, *The Lion On the Path and Other African Stories*. For little children, the telling by Johnny Morris of *The Railway Stories* is delightful. Little Tim, Borka, Humbert and Babar are all available on records.

In foreign languages *French for Fun* is issued by Linguaphone, there are two books and records. There is also a series issued by European School Books including German, Italian, Spanish and French. The latter is entitled *Bonjour Mes Enfants*. Where there is a non-English-speaking community, records in which English is the foreign language might also be provided.

The appearance of the stock of a public library has undergone a revolution since the emergence of the plastic jacket. I remember as a child being disconcerted by the rows of library bindings, but sometimes delighted by the story inside. The preservation of the dust jacket has done a great deal to make our libraries gay and attractive, and it is the jacket which frequently sells the book to our readers. Little rebinding is carried out in most children's libraries today, unless the book is out of print and worth preserving, expensive, or required permanently in the reserve stock. Many books are available in a reinforced binding, and this service is particularly useful for picture books which need to stand up to hard wear, but the insides of many books become dirty before the binding is worn out. A plastic jacket fitted by a supplier at a small charge is extremely good value and sufficient protection for much of the stock.

The senior children's librarian will also be responsible for the supervision and training of staff. She should be present at the interviews of all who are to work in the department. It should be stressed that there is plenty of enjoyment to be found in this work but that it can be exhausting. A considerable amount of reading is necessary both of adult and children's books, and a keen librarian may well get involved with other activities which can take up a great deal of free time. Schools issue invitations to concerts, open days and prize-givings, and like the children's librarian to give talks at parent-teacher meetings. At Christmas and at the end of the summer term, care must be taken that invitations to all schools are accepted by at least one representative of the staff, as teachers will naturally be offended if several people turn up to one and nobody to another. There are meetings about play areas, facilities for the under fives, mothers' clubs, open evenings at youth centres, and children's librarians are invited to talk at courses for teachers, playgroup leaders and nursery nurses. All these talks have to be prepared and even if time in lieu is accepted for extra work, the children's librarian who is on the rota of a busy library and entertaining classes of schoolchildren during the day may have considerable difficulty in finding time to take it. Large systems where the senior children's librarian is not involved in the day-to-day timetable are fortunate, for she will be free to represent the library and visit youth centres, playgroups and training centres and will have the opportunity to stimulate interest in the library. It is also necessary to stress to qualified staff when they are working in a children's room that, unless the branch staff is integrated, it is not always possible to divide the work into professional and non-professional categories completely, and to cover extended opening hours. Some resentment is felt that a qualified children's librarian will be expected to shelve books, which would not be done by a librarian in a large adult department.

A proportion of the assistants are possibly awaiting courses at schools of librarianship and intend to specialize in work with children, or the library may have a trainee system. Formal or informal trainees should be given the opportunity of attending book selection meetings and of discussing with the librarian, in whose area of library they work, which books to select, and they should also take part in the book-reviewing scheme. The best training for an inexperienced librarian or a pre-professional is day-to-day contact in a busy children's library with an experienced children's librarian, learning to use books with children both by observation and development of her own ideas, with help and guidance as necessary.

Courses are organized in some libraries on story-telling and running library clubs, on giving book talks and introductory talks about the library. This is particularly necessary when the member of staff is to work on her own and has not previously been trained. Shropshire has organized special courses for assistants to run library activities in branch libraries during the summer holidays. Possibly neighbouring authorities can co-operate with each other in courses for new staff. Branches of the Youth Libraries Group organize day courses but these are more general. Short courses are now run for staff who have been qualified for some years, on a higher level than the weekend school, in library schools and universities, to stress new developments in education, literature, librarianship and management. The International Summer Schools at Loughborough and the courses at Exeter on children's literature were the preliminary steps in the right direction, and librarians should take any opportunity of attending management courses organized for them. An excellent short course was held in spring 1971 by Leeds School of Librarianship for senior children's librarians on *Recent Developments in Children's Librarianship*.

Students are leaving library schools with a basic knowledge of children's literature and librarianship, but with a lack of experience. The Youth Libraries Group set up a working party to assess the current position in the training of librarians to work with young people. It issued a memorandum which was published in March, 1970,[12] and librarians were invited to make their comments.

It discussed the need for the junior professional to receive a good general training in all departments in an in-service training period of not less than a year. The librarian should have a good working knowledge of general library management, staff supervision, readers' advisory services and the use of bibliographical materials. This is relevant to *A Report on the Supply and Training of Librarians*, 1968, by the Library Advisory Councils, Department of Education and Science.[13]

The memorandum stressed that on appointment to a specialized post the librarian should work under the direction of a senior children's librarian and should take part in an in-service training programme covering all areas of duty, and that advanced courses should be organized for more experienced children's librarians. These could include assessment of books and other material, psychology, educational techniques and the needs of special groups of children. It also suggested that the senior children's librarian should participate in senior general training especially management, and other librarians working mainly in the adult field should be welcome to participate in the initial training scheme for new children's librarians and the further specialist training for senior children's librarians. The initial training scheme could be operated on a co-operative basis where there were insufficient senior staff to make this practical and the need to establish training officers was discussed.

Training officers are being employed by a few public libraries and are responsible for the in-service training of staff and for arranging programmes for students. Education courses are run in several libraries for new staff. Hertfordshire expects all its professional staff to do some children's work and holds ambitious training programmes, including refresher courses and a weekend residential course on work with children. It also has a film of the county library which is used as part of its course.

Assistants working in a lending library may be required to work on their own in a children's room. A talk on principles, routines and library services for children is insufficient and they need at least a couple of days, and preferably a week, working with a children's librarian to learn how to cope with children and their enquiries and to find their way round the book stock. A library will be judged by the enthusiasm and co-operation of the member of staff on duty when help is required. The assistant must know the type of request which cannot be answered immediately but which should be referred to the children's librarian the following day. There should, in a large system, be someone she can reach on the telephone to ask advice about a particular enquiry which through inexperience she cannot answer. It is of little use having an excellent book stock and a reliable and experienced children's librarian, if when she is off duty there is no one on the staff capable of carrying on the service at a high standard.

Children's librarians at all levels should be valued members of the senior staff. It is essential that they have an intelligent interest and that they co-operate in the running of the library as a whole, suggesting new ideas and welcoming constructive criticism of their own service. Organization and method surveys have recently suggested that children's librarians in municipal boroughs should come under the branch or district librarian concerned. With tactful co-operation and a desire for mutual assistance this can work well, providing the senior children's librarian retains overall responsibility for book selection, stock revision and training of staff and advises on the layout and equipment of the children's libraries and on service to children

and schools. The senior children's librarian must be a departmental head on equal terms with other departmental heads.
District librarians who are equally interested in all services in
their area have a balanced judgment of future needs and
development. Children's librarians through direct participation
and shared responsibility for the area concerned, may have
better opportunities than at present to progress to a position of
branch or district librarian without previously transferring to
the adult department, if they wish to broaden their experience.

REFERENCES

1 Ministry of Education. *The Structure of the Public Library Service in England
and Wales*. London, HMSO, 1959 (Roberts Report).

2 Ministry of Education. *Standards of Public Library Service in England and
Wales*. London, HMSO, 1962 (Bourdillion Report).

3 W. C. Berwick Sayers. *A Manual of Children's Libraries*. London, Allen
and Unwin and the Library Association, 1932.

4 International Federation of Library Associations. *Standards of Public
Library Service – Library Premises*. (Memorandum approved in principle at
Warsaw, 1959.) Extracts and working party comments in Appendix 3,
the Bourdillion Report (see note 2 above).

5 Library Association. *Public Library Buildings The Way Ahead*. London
Library Association, 1960. Extracts and working party comments in
Appendix 3, the Bourdillion Report (see note 2 above).

6 Aase Bredsdorff. 'The Danish Standards for Bookstocks and Accessions
II: Children's Departments'. *Scandinavian Public Library Quarterly*, vol. 2,
no. 2, 1969, pp. 87–101. Also appears as abstract in *Library and Information
Science Abstracts*, no. 69/1660, July–August, 1969.

7 Peggy Heeks. *Administration of Children's Libraries*. London, Library
Association, pamphlet no. 30, 1967.

8 Frederick Hallworth. 'Library Service to Schools, Practice in a County'.
Library World, vol. 69, no. 810, December 1967. pp. 150–4.

9 School of Librarianship, North Western Polytechnic. One-day conference on *The Library Market for Children's Books*, 1966. Paper by Anne
Benson on 'Children's Bookselling'.

10 Ibid. Paper by W. H. S. Whitehouse on 'Library Supply and Children's
Books'.

11 Lillian H. Smith. *The Unreluctant Years: A Critical Approach to Children's
Literature*. Chicago, American Library Association, 1953.

12 Youth Libraries Group. 'The Memorandum of the Working Party Set
Up by the Committee To Assess the Current Position of Training for
Library Work with Young People. Post Examination Training for Children's Librarianship'. *Library Association Record*, vol. 72, no. 3, March 1970.
pp. 106–107.

13 Department of Education and Science. *A Report on the Supply and Training of Librarians by the Library Advisory Council (England) and the Library Advisory Council (Wales)*. London, HMSO, 1968.

FURTHER READING

Gask, Catherine. 'Art Reference Library for Children'. *Top of the News*, vol. 11, November 1965. pp. 93–5.

Gross, Elizabeth H. 'The Teaching of Children's Literature'. *Wilson Library Bulletin*, October 1967. pp. 199–205.

Kilpatrick, Elizabeth Gross. 'Do We Need New Directions'. *Top of the News*, vol. 24, June 1968. pp. 399–406.

McBride, Mary. 'In-Service Training of Children's Librarians'. *Youth Library Group News*, February 1969.

Parker, Ann. 'Training for Work with Children in Hertfordshire County Library'. *Youth Library Group News*, February 1969.

RECOMMENDED BOOKS

Arkley, Arthur J. *The Hamish Hamilton Children's Dictionary*. London, Hamish Hamilton, 1964.

Blishen, Edward (ed.). *The Oxford Book of Poetry*. Illustrated by Brian Wildsmith. London, Oxford University Press, 1963.

Burton, Hester. *Castors Away*. London, Oxford University Press, 1962.

Chamber's Children's Illustrated Dictionary. London, W. R. Chambers, 1958.

Children's Britannica. 2nd edition. 20 vols. Encyclopaedia Britannica, 1969.

Cresswell, Helen. *The Night Watchmen*. London, Faber, 1969.

Denny, Norman, and Josephine Filmer-Sankey. *The Bayeux Tapestry*. London, Collins, 1966.

Garner, Alan. *Elidor*. London, Collins, 1965.

Guinness Book of Records. Guinness. Annual.

Hodges, C. Walter. *Shakespeare's Theatre*. London, Oxford University Press, 1964.

Junior Pears Encyclopaedia. Pelham Books Ltd. Annual.

Leutscher, Alfred. *Life in Fresh Waters*. Natural Science Picture Books. London, The Bodley Head, 1964.

Mayne, William. *Earth Fasts*. London, Hamish Hamilton, 1966.

Oxford Junior Encyclopaedia. 2nd edition. 13 vols. London, Oxford University Press, 1964.

Robinson, Veronica. *David in Silence*. London, Deutsch, 1965.

Swinton, W. E. *Digging for Dinosaurs*. Natural Science Picture Books. London, The Bodley Head, 1962.

Thorndike, E. L. *Junior Illustrated Dictionary*. London, University of London Press, 1947.

Treece, Henry. *The Dream-Time*. London, Brockhampton, 1967.
Untermeyer, Louis. *The Golden Treasury of Poetry*. London, Collins, 1961.
Vevers, Gwynne. *Life in the Sea*. Natural Science Picture Books. London, The Bodley Head, 1963.
Whitaker's Almanack. Whitakers. Annual.
Who's Who. Black. Annual.

RECOMMENDED PERIODICALS

Aeromodeller. Model and Allied Publications Ltd. Monthly.
Animals. N. Sitwell. Monthly.
Children's Book Review. Five Owls Press Ltd. Six issues a year.
Children's Literature in Education. Ward Lock Educational. Three issues a year.
Elizabethan. Elizabethan. Monthly.
Growing Point. Margery Fisher, Ashton Manor, Northampton, England. Nine issues yearly.
Junior Bookshelf. Marsh Hall, Thurstonland, Huddersfield. Six issues a year.
Meccano Magazine. Model and Allied Publications Ltd. Monthly.
Pictorial Education. Evans. Monthly and quarterly.
Puffin Post. Penguin Books Ltd. Quarterly.
School Librarian. Premier House, 150 Southampton Row, WC1. Four times a year.
Signal. The Thimble Press, Stroud, Glos. Three issues a year.
The Times Educational Supplement. Weekly.
The Times Literary Supplement. Children's book supplement. Four times a year.

RECOMMENDED RECORDS

Ardizzone, Edward. *Little Tim Stories*. Read by David Davis. Delyse. Del 128.
Awdry, W. *The Railway Stories*. Read by Johnny Morris. Delyse. Del 137–142.
Belloc, Hilaire. *Cautionary Verses*. Read by Peter Ustinov. Argo. RG 599.
Britten, Benjamin. *Let's Make An Opera*. Decca. LXT 5163.
Britten, Benjamin. *The Young Person's Guide to the Orchestra*. Decca Ace of Clubs. ACL 30.
Brunhoff, Jean de. *Babar the Elephant*. Read by Peter Ustinov. EMI. ALP 2286.
Burningham, John. *Humbert and Borka*. Read by Eric Thompson. Delyse. Del 772.
Eliot, T. S. *Old Possum's Book of Practical Cats*. ARGO. RG 116.
European Schoolbooks Ltd. *Bonjour, Mes Enfants!* MAF records 1–6.
Grimm. *The Story of the Little Tailor*. Read by Peter Ustinov. EMI. ALP 2286.
The Lion on the Path and Other African Stories told by Hugh Tracey. Music of Africa series. Decca. LK 4914.

Linguaphone Sonodisc. *French for Fun*. Sonodisc Ltd. SON FFI/A–FFI/F.
Poetry and Song. Argo in association with Macmillan. DA 50–63.
Prokofiev, Serge. *Peter and the Wolf*. Decca Ace of Clubs. ACL 30.
Rhyme and Rhythm. Argo in association with Macmillan. PLP 1077–1080.
Saint-Saëns, Camille. *Carnival of the Animals*. Ravel (Daphnis) Telefunken. GMA 41.

Chapter 5
Routine Processes

A children's librarian in her first and subsequent posts will usually find the routine processes well established, although these must be changed from time to time to become more efficient or to meet new developments. However, when establishing a new service, particularly in developing countries, or even with amalgamation of existing authorities, different methods will have to be compared, new routines evolved and stationery will need to be designed by the children's librarian concerned.

Registration is necessary for all members of the public wishing to use the library. A child is usually entitled to have a reader's card or tickets if he is either a resident or attending school within the local authority area. Reciprocal arrangements are normally in force and tickets obtained from another system may be used in the library chosen by the child. It is idealistic, but I should like to see library facilities throughout the country immediately available on signature of an application form wherever the applicant lived or worked. In practice some libraries hold small stocks of a neighbouring authority's application cards and post them to the library concerned asking the other authority to forward the tickets. This happens particularly when the library is nearer the homes of the children concerned, and at her discretion the librarian may allow the children to take books in anticipation of the tickets arriving.

When a child can read and write it is a good idea for him to sign a simple statement that he wishes to join the library and will look after any materials borrowed.

The reverse of the card should be signed by the parent, guardian or teacher. It is a good idea for application cards to be taken home to be signed by the parent before a class visit, so the cards should be sent in advance to the school. The parent is then aware that the child has books in his possession and will

Figure 1

Specimen Reader's Voucher

ADALTON LIBRARIES

I wish to become a member of the Adalton Libraries and I
promise to take care of the books/gramophone records I
borrow and to return them punctually to the Library

Name (in full) . . . .
                    BLOCK LETTERS

Home Address . . . .

School . . . .   Age . . . .

Date . . . .   No. of tickets issued . . . .

                                    Date of expiry . . . .

---

help look after them. If a parent refuses to allow the child to
take books home the teacher is usually happy to sign the card
and arrange for the child to read his books in school. When
teachers sign an undertaking that they believe the child to be
reliable it should be made clear that they will not be financially
responsible for any book lost or damaged.

At East York Library and Toronto Public Libraries children
were allowed to take a book home in anticipation of their card
being signed by their parent. This was a good idea in that the
child's interest and enthusiasm could be satisfied immediately
but very occasionally disappointment arose when parents
refused, although arrangements could always be made for the
child to have books in school. A difficulty arises when a family
have recently moved into the area and the parent is not yet on
the electoral role and he cannot produce a rate demand as rates
are included in the rent. The children's librarian prefers the
signature of the parent to that of any ratepayer who may not
know the family well, so the parent signs the child's form, only

to find that in the adult library he must himself have a guarantor. This is poor public relations and a rent book or connection letter for gas, electricity or telephone sent through the post should be adequate proof of residence, if really required.

When a child asks to join the library his name should be checked to see if he is already a member, if the authority keeps a borrowers' register. He may have forgotten he had previously left his tickets for safe keeping at the library, or he may have lost them, or he may have failed to return books previously. Frequently the books will be brought back or paid for if the child is tackled gently when he is trying to join again. When the event has occurred some years before, rather than deprive the child of books it is better to let it be a warning to him and allow him to join again, although it may be wise to limit the number of tickets for a little while. Some libraries circulate lists of defaulters or register these centrally, so that defaulters are recorded and noticed when they subsequently attempt to rejoin.

Figure 2

Sample Bookcard

Accessions Number	
Class Number	
Author	
Title	
Price	

Keen readers may register at two or more libraries. As long as they return the books promptly to the right library there is no reason to prevent this.

The type of ticket a child will receive will depend on the charging system in use. The Browne charging method is popular in children's libraries where it is not necessary to get a large number of children in and out of a room in a short period. Each book in the library will have a bookcard on the top of which will be an accession number or symbol to identify it, and its class number, author and title.

The child will be given a number of tickets, usually between two and four, according to the available book stock and its use. Some authorities restrict young children to two books as they feel that picture books are expensive and two are enough for a young child to take care of. Others feel that they should have more as they are read quickly, even though many young children like to hear the same story again, and because it may be difficult for mothers to have to keep coming to the library. The child's tickets will show his name, his address, symbol or name of the branch he uses, and the date when his tickets expire. It will be made in the shape of a pocket so that the bookcard can be enclosed. When the child takes a book out the card will be taken out of the book and filed inside the child's ticket and filed in sequence behind the date-due-back slip. There will also be a label in the book where the date for return is stamped. Class loans can all be kept under the name of the teacher, but with the bookcard inside the child's ticket to save time in discharging if necessary.

It is convenient if the period of loan can be the same in all departments so that all books borrowed in a family at the same time are due back together. With Browne it is simple to know what books a child has borrowed once his tickets are found in the issue and whether he has lost a ticket or a book. Files must be kept of temporary tickets and bookcards for any not found when the book is returned. Browne is a quick method for charging books but slow for discharging.

Token charging is used in libraries where speed is essential. It is cheaper to use tokens than employ additional staff for busy periods. The child may be given a reader's card (although some libraries do not issue these) with his name, address, date of expiry and number, and a given number of tokens. As he takes out a book he shows his reader's card, the token is handed in, a date due card put in the pocket or a label stamped. When the book is returned he is given a token. It is extremely quick both in taking out and returning books to the library, and the number of books borrowed is limited. Stock control is difficult; it is impossible to tell whether a book is missing or in frequent demand. It is not possible to search the issue, so reserves have to be checked on a visible index and copies borrowed which are on the shelves of other libraries or purchased. Nor is it possible to tell whether a child has lost a book or token, and legality has been questioned when charges have been made for lost tokens. When a book is missing it is not possible to tell the child the name of the book or show him another copy or describe it so that he knows what he is looking for. An adaptation of the token system is to make out and hold children's tickets while they have books out. As long as they return and take out the same number of books they are handed tokens which must not be taken out of the library. If they hand in a token without taking a book they are given their ticket. Registration is slightly slower than in the normal token method as tickets have to be made out and charging is slower if children do not take out the same number of books. Notices telling children not to take tokens home must be placed on the tokens and by the door of the library. Any token method is bound to be based fundamentally on trust and a child cannot be charged for a lost book unless it is definite that he has had it. A fair standard price is also difficult to arrive at for, say, a Beatrix Potter compared with a Cassell Caravel. Some leeway is necessary in cases of hardship or when the reader knows the title of the missing book, which may be replaced at a lower price than the standard one.

In photocharging the child will have a reader's card which will state his name, address and date of expiry, or alternatively date of issue. Following an experiment at Wandsworth, Mr E. V. Corbett suggested they should be made of white xylonite with a matt surface.[1] A bookcard is sometimes used but it is more economical to put the accession number on the flyleaf and photograph that with the reader's card and transaction card. The transaction card is numbered and pre-stamped with the date due for return and is put inside a pocket in the book. When the book is returned the transaction card is taken out of the book and stored carefully. Later any numbers of transaction cards which are missing from the sequence will be checked on the film and overdues can be sent. A stock register of books in accession number order is necessary unless the author and title is put on the flyleaf of the book with the accession number. It must be stressed to children that they must leave the transaction card in the book. The advantages of this method are that it gives an accurate record of what the reader has out, but the only way of checking overdues or queries is by reading the film. Photocharging is faster than Browne for discharging although not for charging. Reserves have to be searched for, which is less satisfactory than stopping in the issue and it is possible for children to take out more books than allowed. Children sometimes think there is some mystique about this method and one little boy once told me very seriously that he could not take an extra book because the machine had his picture.

Figure 3

Specimen Transaction Card

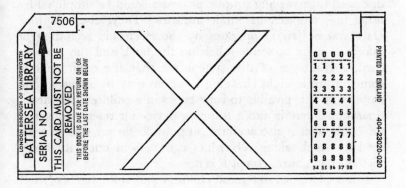

Figure 4

Specimen Reader's Card

```
WANDSWORTH PUBLIC LIBRARIES
BATTERSEA DISTRICT LIBRARY, S.W.11


Name ...............................


Address ...........................

.....................................

Issued ...............................
MEMBERSHIP CARD
(Available only in Wandsworth Libraries)
```

The most recent methods of charging utilize the local authority computers. R. T. Kimber in *Program,* October 1968,[2] described the method used at Chichester. The reader and the book have small edge-punched cards which are mechanically read at the library counter. Paper tape is punched for books taken out and returned. A weekly computer run updates the master loan file and prints overdues. W. S. H. Ashmore in an article in 1969 discussed how varying routine processes could be simplified by using the computer in public libraries.[3] The Plessey Capture Data system (1971) operates by the electronic recording of information on adhesive labels on the book and the reader's card. Advantages of this system are that the equipment is compact, up to eight charging locations may be linked to one cassette, so it is possible to issue books in a children's library if desirable. There is also a trapping device for reservations and the equipment is also available in portable form which may be used for stock-taking. Overdues can be sent out with every method mentioned except token.

It is a good idea to remind children they still have books out so that there is less chance of them becoming lost. When the library sends overdues will depend on the authority but it is probably wise to leave them until the books are about two or three weeks overdue. The first overdue may be sent to the child.

Figure 5

Specimen First Overdue

```
┌─────────────────────────────────────────────────────────┐
│                   ADALTON LIBRARIES                       │
│                                                           │
│                                    Date as postmark       │
│                                                           │
│  ........................................................  │
│                                                           │
│  ........................................................  │
│                                                           │
│  ........................................................  │
│                                                           │
│  ........................................................  │
│                                                           │
│  Please return the above book(s) due back on ............ │
│  No charge is made for overdue children's books and you are asked │
│  to return your books promptly so that others may read them. │
└─────────────────────────────────────────────────────────┘
```

Figure 6

Specimen Overdue to Parent

```
┌─────────────────────────────────────────────────────────┐
│                   ADALTON LIBRARIES                       │
│                                                           │
│                                    Date as postmark       │
│                                                           │
│  ........................................................  │
│                                                           │
│  ........................................................  │
│                                                           │
│  ........................................................  │
│                                                           │
│  ........................................................  │
│                                                           │
│  Would you please ask ............. to return the above  │
│  book(s) immediately. No charge is made for overdue children's │
│  books.                                                   │
└─────────────────────────────────────────────────────────┘
```

If a book is still not returned after a further two weeks a reminder postcard may be sent to the parent or guardian who signed the child's registration card. If the child comes with a school class and the application card was signed by the teacher it is better to talk to the child when he comes to the library. If sending overdues to parents is considered undesirable a second card may be sent to the child.

Some libraries send porters to collect books which are not returned and this is often satisfactory. An account listing the books missing with a price against them, but also stating that return of books will cancel the account will bring a lot of books back. The price set on a lost or damaged book must not be so high as to prevent children from continuing to use the service. A guide as a maximum might be seventy-five per cent in the first year after purchase, fifty per cent in the second year and twenty-five per cent in subsequent years, but allowing the librarian's discretion to reduce this. The children's librarian will know the area and probably the child concerned, and, except in rare cases of persistent damage, a child should not be deprived of the opportunity to have books in his home.

Children should be given the opportunity to reserve books which are in the stock of the library, and suggestions for books not in stock should be considered for purchase on their merit. It is undesirable to charge for reserving books and if the service is abused the number of reservation cards may be limited. Some libraries put the names or cards of children on the noticeboard when they have books to be collected. This relies on bush telegraph or on the child visiting the library very regularly, and looks untidy. A more efficient method is to tell them through the post. It is necessary to ensure with children, when they reserve a book, that the book will still be wanted at a later date and that they will collect it.

Some books may have to be borrowed from another library in the system and an inter-branch form may be required. It is useful if the branch indicates whether they would like a copy purchased.

In the Roberts Report it was stated that fines should not be levied in children's libraries. Fines may prevent books from being returned, and children may be deprived of a service because parents refuse to pay a fine. This report was opposed

Figure 7

Specimen Reservation Card

ADALTON LIBRARIES

Date as postmark

Author ....

Title ....

.... Subject no. ....

This book will be kept for you until ....
When you come to collect it, please bring this card and a library
book or ticket with you.

---

to charging for any material borrowed from the public library.[4]
But the concept of the free library service is under fire at present.
It is to be hoped that whatever the outcome it will remain a
free service to children and old people.

Ordering of Books

Books may be ordered from suppliers on cards, typed lists,
suppliers' slips or catalogues. The library will need a record of
each title ordered which is usually filed on 5in. × 3in. cards,
and includes the following details: author, title, publisher,
edition, date and price. It should also indicate the firm from
which the book is on order, date of order, and signify which
libraries require it.

This card may be used later as the master record, and if a
card or slip is sent to the supplier it should be possible to keep a
carbon copy. When the books are received, the file card is
removed from the on-order file, books are accessioned, the price
of each book is checked with the invoice and providing all is in
order the invoice is approved, dated and the accession numbers
used are put on the invoice and in the accession register, if this is

used. Local auditors require some method of linking up a book to an order so that it can be found in stock if necessary.

Children's books are usually separated on library shelves into picture books, under nines, fiction, non-fiction, and sometimes books for older readers. ITA and books for backward readers may also be shelved separately. It is not the purpose here to discuss the theory and practice of classification, but books must be placed on shelves in such a way that related subjects are together and can be found and replaced speedily. The Dewey Decimal Scheme is normally used in adult libraries in Britain so children will find it easier if children's and school libraries are classified by Dewey also. It does have disadvantages in that it separates such related subjects as armour and medieval history and different aspects of the same subject, e.g. transport into economics and engineering, but books are more complex than the logical divisions of the classification scheme. There is a simplified edition of Dewey for schools, the 15th edition, which is useful. As far as possible the classification numbers in adult, junior, and school libraries should correspond, though numbers should be shortened for children's books. It is better to form authority tables based on a definite edition of Dewey and make notes under the schedule. New subjects should be written in and discussed with the classifier of adult books if they are separately dealt with to be as consistent as possible. Toronto has a scheme which was devised under very broad subject headings and with an alphabetical notation to follow a natural progression of a child's reading interests, and there is also the Cheltenham Classification Scheme based on a similar principle. With an increased number of books Toronto's scheme has been further subdivided in recent years. The book knowledge of the children's librarians there is superb and they know exactly what a book looks like and what information they will find in it. Less highly trained librarians elsewhere rely heavily on their particular classification scheme for help.

A subject index with the classification schedules is essential for members of staff in branches, and a subject index should be made for the children's use, unless there is a dictionary catalogue. The visible panels, either on a stand or fitted to a wall, are popular and additional strips may be put in as necessary. Children enjoy using these, and they are more satisfactory than a subject index or subject entry in a dictionary card catalogue.

It is not universally accepted that catalogues are necessary in a children's library (or for fiction in an adult library), or that the expense involved is justified, and some children's libraries appear to run efficiently without them. It is also argued that unless the book is available there is little point in knowing about it!

Bibliographies such as *Books in Print* can be used to find an author if the child has the right title. New titles cannot be found here and non-fiction is more difficult if the correct title is not known. New staff and staff on relief find a catalogue reassuring, and may find books on the shelves which otherwise would not come to light while the reader was there. On the other hand, Camden has a computer catalogue which co-ordinates the stock of all the children's libraries giving locations. If a book required is out of one library it is possible to telex (if installed) or telephone other libraries until a copy is located; which is an invaluable service. Catalogue cards may be purchased from the British National Bibliography but it may be necessary to adapt classification numbers. Library suppliers produce as a service catalogue entries, the library supplying the cards. It is necessary to check these, particularly for author headings and date of publication.

Catalogues may be in varying forms: author and title for fiction, author and classified for non-fiction, and the author catalogue for both fiction and non-fiction may be in one sequence. There may be one sequence for author, title and subject – a dictionary catalogue. We should not force children to use a catalogue. Teenagers in the United States have complained that public libraries place too much emphasis on the use of the catalogue, but young people will be at a disadvantage in a busy adult library if they do not understand how one works.

When children come to the library the staff and the routines are there to serve them. To be inflexible and never bend a regulation when justified detracts from the image of a library as a happy and lively place.

REFERENCES

1 Edmund V. Corbett. *Photo-Charging: Its Operation and Installation in a British Public Library*. London, J. Clarke, 1957.
2 R. T. Kimber. 'An Operational Computerized Circulation System with On-line Interrogation Capability'. *Program*, vol. 2, no. 3, October 1968. pp. 75–80. Abstract: *Library and Information Science Abstracts*, January–February 1969. Ref. 62/296.
3 W. S. H. Ashmore. 'An Integrated Computer System for Public Libraries'. *Journal of Librarianship*, vol. 1, no. 4, October 1969. pp. 253–63.
4 Ministry of Education. *The Structure of the Public Library Service in England and Wales* (Roberts Report). London, HMSO, 1959.

Chapter 6
The Library and the Individual Child

The best advertisement of a library service to the individual child is by word of mouth. Nothing succeeds like success and a happy member will often pass on his books to other children, and suggest they should join too. The old idea of a lower age limit is dying, but not fast enough, and more mothers at home with little children are realizing the value of picture books in their children's development. They bring their children to the library and are encouraging their friends to bring their children too. The best way to exploit the stock is by personal recommendation.

The relationship between a child and a librarian should be intimate and the child should be aware that the librarian is always willing to help him if he wants her to. Help must be given tactfully and children must be allowed to have the pleasure of browsing if they wish. Nor should a book the librarian considers inappropriate to the age of the child be replaced by something more suitable. It is perhaps advisable to say that you think he might enjoy it more in a year or two and to ask if he would like to change it. If not, tell him to bring it back and get something else if he does not like it. Be prepared, however, for him to come back somewhat defiantly as a six-year-old once did who said he had read every word of *Knight Crusader* by Ronald Welch. Fortunately that time there was another book in with a knight on the dust cover, *The Little Knight's Dragon* by Denise and Alain Trez and so I was able to give him this. If a child is allowed to take three or four books home, one unsatisfactory one will not be such a disappointment.

A librarian working with children and selecting books for her library must know her stock. An accumulation of book knowledge builds up over the years but it is necessary to read widely covering a broad range of fiction and non-fiction for all abilities so that books can be recommended that have actually been read. Neither should she neglect reading adult books. It is not unknown for children's librarians to feel guilty if they read adult books at home as there are so many children's books to read, but some time at work should also be set aside for this especially for newer members of staff.

If children ask about a book which you have not read it is best to tell them so. When the system has a book-reviewing scheme and the book has been seen and discussed with the reviewer at a book meeting, you can tell the child a little about it and that, say, Mrs Long at Riverview read it and thought it was good, but if he takes it ask him to tell you what he thinks about it. Children also recommend books to each other, and a few libraries have magazines which incorporate reviews by children. At primary school age children are usually better at talking about the book than writing their thoughts down. Question and answer sessions with an author are enjoyed. Older children are more objective and critical in their approach and Toronto Public Libraries produce an excellent magazine of reviews by young people called *Opinion*. The child should be shown that the librarian is there to help him and he should never be reluctant to ask for help. A member of the staff should walk around the room in busy periods so that she is readily available and can see if children need help. If there is only one person on duty, completely occupied with the mechanics of charging and discharging books, the standard of service is poor. When charging is at a central desk it is usually preferable to register readers in the children's library. The children's librarian meets the child, can show him the arrangement of the library, or take him to the younger children's section and offer help in finding books if he is small.

Most of us are horrified at times with the limitations of our own knowledge and it is important to find out exactly what the child wants. It is far better if you don't know to tell him so and ask him to describe what he wants rather than send him away disappointed. On one of my first days in Toronto a small group of Italian girls of about eleven years old came into the library after school and asked me for *Old Faithful*. Not knowing American books I asked if it was a horse or dog story – with glee they assured me it was a geyser in Yellowstone Park.

When children are doing homework or working on topics, the

library staff must take care that the child finds the information himself. The librarian may show the child which books to look in and how to use the index but on no account should she do the work for the child. Quizzes given to children to do during school holidays are sometimes extremely hard for the age group for which they are set, and one wonders whether the teachers concerned have looked up the information for themselves. A quiz on local history and civics asked for the number of fire engines in a particular town. The children called at and also telephoned the station who referred them to the library, but it was an extremely thoughtless question.

As librarians engaged in work with children in a library or administering a service for them, our work is to stimulate and satisfy a desire for knowledge and enjoyment through books and all other media at our disposal. There are two essential factors to be considered, the stock and the staff.

Is the stock carefully selected and adequate to cope with the increased use which should follow publicity? Are there sufficient funds to purchase in quantity selected new material and to replace existing stock as required? The *Public Library Statistics* illustrate the disparity in the number of children's books purchased between places of similar population.[1] Nor does it appear that the Bourdillion standard of 1,500 titles added a year had been implemented.[2] The 1964 Public Libraries Act[3] followed the comments of the Roberts Committee[4] that authorities under 40,000 population may not be viable and should be subject to review. However, the redistribution of local authority boundaries in 1974 will result in larger library authorities.

Another question to ask is: are all the staff, both at the service-points and in administrative positions, keen and have they had sufficient internal and, if appropriate, professional training to make the library a cultural and educational force in the community? We should not be satisfied just to lend books to people who come to us of their own accord. This is far too narrow. The community should be made aware of our existence and purpose by librarians going out into the community and using all available avenues of communication.

Librarians should accept, and indeed initiate, invitations to visit mothers' clubs, housebound housewives' associations, church clubs and Women's Institutes to discuss books for their children and the services for children and adults the library offers. It is a good idea to take book lists and a small collection of books with you including paperbacks so that parents can be made aware of what is on the market and available in libraries. It is useful to leave a small collection of books with the group for about a month so that they can circulate in the homes of the families. Plenty of time should be allowed for questions; favourite ones are about violence in fairytales, and the policy the library has in book selection. The acceptance of violence in stories and legends depends on how the author presents it and on how a story-teller or reader tells the tale. A normal child in a secure environment gradually learns to distinguish between the real and the imaginary. These tales are best avoided for a very young child. If there is anything that may be frightening in a story, it is essential that someone who is close to the child, preferably one of his parents, should be there to comfort him. Emotions experienced through stories will help the child to understand and control his developing feelings towards the world around him. Children have their own fears which are probably more real than anything in a book, and in many homes there is clearly an opportunity to see and hear violence on the television screens. Nicholas Tucker wrote an excellent article on this subject in *Where*.[5]

When book selection is discussed parents are usually amazed to hear the number of children's books published each year. It is a good idea to tell them approximately how many books are purchased and for how many libraries and schools. It is usually appreciated that it is only possible to buy a certain proportion of what is available and that the cheap, crudely illustrated and poorly produced books, especially for younger children, cannot be compared with the beautiful illustrated books of, for example, Helen Oxenbury, Brian Wildsmith and Charles Keeping. Modern writers of the calibre of Alan Garner, Leon Garfield and Hester Burton should be contrasted with writers who were once fashionable. An article by Edward Blishen in *Where*[6] and the collection *Young Writers, Young Readers*, edited by Boris Ford,[7] are useful to refer to.

The library is a useful meeting-place for a local branch of the Federation of Book Groups, and through talks to parents may even be instrumental in starting one. Arrangements can be made for parents to view some of the new books. Many libraries have held meetings for parents at which an author or critic has talked on children's books. A Children's Book Group could form the nucleus of a talk like this.

Guides to the library service are invaluable; in a large system there may be one for each department, but a smaller system will have one which will incorporate all services. The guide should state which materials are available, give information on the eligibility of tickets, how many are allowed, and whether the card should be signed by the parent or, in the case of non-residents, by the teacher. Simple advice should be given on the arrangement of books on the shelves and activities in the library. The libraries' addresses should be shown, hours of opening, telephone numbers and in cities where the position of different libraries may not be known a map could show them. The guide can be given to each child as he joins the library and also sent to schools, playgroups and clinics. It is essential that they are regularly revised and kept up to date.

When a new library is being opened a printed letter, which is either posted or distributed from door to door, should introduce it to the local residents. The letter should state what services the new library is to offer and whether they are for adults and children. It should give information about eligibility for tickets and possibly state, if it is still appropriate, that it is a free service. When a library was opened as part of a housing redevelopment scheme in Central London it was horrifying to discover how many adults did not know that public libraries are free. Many parents thought it was only free to children if they joined through the school, and were delighted to find that younger children could have books. Now, when the question of the free library service is coming under fire, if charges are implemented, people may deprive themselves and their children of a service that they are afraid will be expensive. The leaflet should include a map showing the location of the library, particularly in areas of new development where there are new residents.

Displays of books should be set up outside the library to attract people who never use it; maternal and child welfare clinics will put up a small stand of books if there is room. They usually agree to display posters advertising the library story hours and to distribute book lists. Books can also be left in clinics for children awaiting treatment; they may have a book-mark inside saying that the book comes from the library and that no one is too young to join – assuming there is no lower age limit. Lists of books for the family to read aloud get into homes from the clinics; they can include picture books, nursery rhymes, poetry and stories that a family will enjoy reading together. Book lists are a good way of bringing selected books to the attention of adults and young people who may be shy about asking for help. They are particularly useful when books are being bought as presents for children, or when, regrettably, there is no specialist or anyone on the staff of a library with a working knowledge of children's books, children's librarians receive letters asking for a book list, for example, for a boy of nine with no indication of what he has previously read or what his interests are. Even when details of a child's interests are known, John Rowe Townsend compared this to the problems of matching couples by computer.[8] School book lists which children are recommended to read before going to a grammar school are sometimes years out of date, and modern authors are omitted. Libraries should welcome the opportunity to produce dated book lists for individuals and schools, and with schools it is worthwhile having multiple copies so that the teacher can give a copy to each child. Needless to say any publicity should be well produced, especially in these days of expert commercial advertising.

Many authorities have produced book lists. Camden in previous years has published some excellent ones including *Smoothing the Path*, one to prepare a child for hospital and the other for school. Other subjects which have been covered are ghosts, Guy Fawkes, the American Civil War, and the Battle of Hastings, and a list was also produced to complement a display of books for playgroups which moved around the branches. An exhibition of books, and a list to accompany it, is frequently set up before Christmas, to encourage adults to buy books for children as presents or children to buy with book tokens. Jennifer Shepherd edited an excellent co-operative list from eight Midland libraries in 1972 and the Youth Libraries Group has a publishing programme producing relevant book lists for children, parents, teachers and librarians. The County Libraries Group has produced in their Readers' Guides some useful lists which include *The Reluctant Reader*, 3rd ed., 1969, and for teenagers, *Attitudes and Adventures*, 3rd ed., 1971.

The School Library Association and the School Library Association in Scotland have each produced useful book lists such as *Historical Novels for Use in Schools*, 1970, and *Books for Primary Children*, 1969, compiled by Berna Clark. Peggy Heeks compiled *Books of Reference for School Libraries*, 2nd edition, 1968. The Association has also published an abridged edition of the Bliss Classification Scheme for use in schools, 1967, and *A Guide to Book-Lists and Bibliographies for the Use of Schools*, compiled by Peter Platt, 3rd edition, 1969.[10]

The National Book League produce book lists regularly when they hold their book exhibitions, and these may be borrowed. A particularly valuable series was on fiction, under the editorship of Jessica Jenkins, and covered fantasy, historical fiction for children and adults, mystery and adventure, children of other lands, animal stories, and after thirteen. Special lists have also been prepared for the National Library Week which include *Growing Up with Books* compiled by Betty Jeffery. Kathleen Lines's list *Four to Fourteen* is still extremely useful but the second edition was published in 1956.

Under the editorship of Nancy Chambers, Elaine Moss compiled the first of four lists in a new series Reading for Enjoyment, which is intended for two- to five-year-olds. Other compilers are Brian Alderson, Jessica Jenkins and Aidan Chambers. The lists are primarily aimed at parents, but surely also have a place in the library and school.

In a children's library book lists should never be considered as an alternative to advising readers. But they are an excellent accompaniment to a display of books or they may advertise books on a particular subject, especially if children have been invited to a talk. Parents will value a list of books to read aloud with the family, and of books to use with young children. Some authorities have a library magazine which is distributed to children in schools and libraries like the *Young Reader* at Islington. Brief annotations are given for books included and these may be articles devoted to the work of one author, or to writers on a particular subject.

Display is vital and can stimulate considerable interest and is important both inside the library and in other places where people congregate. A few authorities who particularly appreciate the value of this work have appointed a display artist and may even have a small display department. The person appointed may be expected to combine the design of publicity and put up displays in the libraries, but the talents required for each job are rather different. Most library staff are required to set up displays, and it is particularly important that a children's room should appear attractive and welcoming. Librarians can get good ideas on display by visiting exhibitions, trade fairs, or a well-displayed museum like those at Leicester or York. Sometimes the ideas are fairly simple, but the use of colour, the angles at which objects are placed, distinctive guiding and subtle use of lights cannot fail to catch the attention of passers-by.

Displays should be changed at monthly intervals and a wide range of topics should be introduced. It is a good idea to include fiction and non-fiction together where possible and to cover a wide ability range. When a display case can be locked it is possible to include original documents from the local history collection; for example, to mark the centenary of the Public Education Act, 1870, admission books, ledgers, reports and pictures could have been shown of any local school which was in existence at that time. Facsimiles of contemporary documents like those supplied in the Jackdaws are useful in historical and scientific displays, and it is an excellent scheme for libraries to arrange to copy material relative to their own local history as has been done in Wiltshire. This will also be extremely useful for teaching in schools.

Exhibits may be borrowed from museums, publishers, individuals and a variety of commercial firms. To heighten interest in her book displays one enterprising children's librarian borrowed camping equipment from the Youth Hostel Association, Victorian toys from Pollock's Toy Museum, a model liner which could be lit up from a shipping company, a portable radio telephone from the Post Office, and a stuffed ocelot.

Excellent posters can be obtained from London Transport, the British Travel Association, national tourist agencies, and the Commonwealth Institute. Some of these will have to be paid for. *The Treasure Chest for Teachers* may give other ideas.

Staff usually have to make their own posters to advertise their own events, and unless the person concerned is good at lettering, letraset should be used. Models and mobiles may be made by staff (books in the handicraft section are useful for this) and can result in effective displays. At Christmas staff go to considerable lengths to decorate the library. A certain limit must be placed on the amount of staff time which is to be put into display work and we should not forget the art work of the children themselves. Older children who help in the library are often extremely glad to be given the opportunity of putting up a display, especially if they can select the subject and materials. Their approach is fresh and imaginative. Little children can draw pictures or make models to be displayed in the room, but display work should not be biased in favour of the under sevens as this can be offputting for older children.

Schools usually welcome the opportunity to lend work for display in the library. A model Roman village did a tour of several libraries as did a book of poetry, written by the children on birds and fishes, which opened up into a frieze of brilliant coloured embroidery of the animals described. When children's work is displayed it encourages children to bring their parents to see it. A group of infants at a school near the Tate Gallery lent the library some spectacular pictures they had painted after a visit there.

Parent-teacher meetings are a valuable means of reaching the parents, some of whom may be completely unaware of the services the library can offer. The value of fiction in a child's development should be discussed, as there are still a number of parents around who think reading is a waste of time unless it is to do with homework. A display of books set up in the hall or entrance hall will complement the talk.

The local press are helpful in covering events in libraries especially when they have to do with children, and will frequently send a photographer if given sufficient notice. Children's librarians sometimes write book reviews for the local press or give a list of new additions to the library. A few library authorities have their own periodical. Interesting articles on books for children appear in the *Camden Journal*, written by publishers, critics, and librarians.

Local radio may also be used to keep people aware of what is happening in the library. New and increased services, concerts,

exhibitions and talks may all be given publicity through interviews with members of staff and the public. Jack Dove suggests
that programmes should take place in the library.[11] Young
people discussing books, records or films would be an excellent
means of exploiting library materials. Oral and visual communication is essential to modern society, and to compete in a
changing world all new media must be exploited to its full
potential.

REFERENCES

1 Institute of Municipal Treasurers and the Society of County Treasurers.
Public Library Statistics. Annual.

2 Ministry of Education. *Standards of Public Library Service in England and
Wales. Report of the Working Party Appointed by the Ministry of Education in
March 1961* (Bourdillion Report). London, HMSO, 1962.

3 Public Libraries and Museum Act, 1964. Elizabeth 2, 1964. London,
HMSO, 1964.

4 Ministry of Education. *The Structure of the Public Library Service in England
and Wales* (Roberts Report). Cmnd. 660, 1959.

5 Nicholas Tucker. 'Books That Frighten', *Where*, supplement 15: Books
for Children. pp. 10–12.

6 Edward Blishen. 'Round Up of Eleven New Authors To Try'. *Where*,
supplement 15: Books for Children. pp. 18–19.

7 Boris Ford (ed.). *Young Writers, Young Readers: An Anthology of Children's
Reading and Writing*. Revised edition. 1963. See especially 'The Work of
Enid Blyton' by Janice Dohm, pp. 99–106, and 'Captain Johns and the
Adult World' by D. R. Barnes, pp. 115–22.

8 John Rowe Townsend. 'Where To Go for Information About Children's
Books'. *Where*, supplement 15: Books for Children. pp. 22–3.

9 *Abridged Bliss Classification . . . Revised for School Libraries by the Bliss
Classification Working Party*. London, School Library Association, 1969.

10 Peter Platt (comp.). *A Guide to Book-Lists and Bibliographies for the Use of
Schools*. 3rd edition. School Library Association, 1969.

11 Jack Dove. 'Local Broadcasting and the Library'. *Library World*, vol. 70,
July 1968. pp. 15–16.

FURTHER READING

Freiser, Leonard H. 'The Civilized Network'. *Library Journal*, September
1967. pp. 3001–3.
Pickard, P. M. *I Could A Tale Unfold*. London, Tavistock, 1961.

Chapter 7
The Public Library and the School

Co-operation with schools is essential in our work in public libraries, whether or not we are responsible for a school library service. It is not the purpose of this book to discuss the library in the school, but I would refer the reader to *The Library Service to Schools* by Sheila Ray which is a useful monograph on this service.[1]

In counties, cities, county boroughs and the Outer London boroughs, the librarian in charge of work with young people is often responsible for service to children both in the public library and in the schools. Other authorities have a completely separate educational service to schools. The Inner London Education Authority is responsible and not the children's librarians of the Inner London boroughs for school libraries in that area. Helpful co-operation is essential between the school librarians, the school library advisers and the children's librarian of the public library. However, when the same area is covered by one authority as in county boroughs and counties (with the exception of any independent library authorities) it is better, as suggested by Sheila Ray, that one person is in control of both services, although it may be necessary in a large authority to delegate a good deal of the work to a specialist staff. In counties where there are independent library authorities within the area the county authorities are responsible for libraries in the schools unless there are any 'excepted districts'.

In rural areas the school may lend books to read at home as the children may live too far away to attend a local branch library, and the mobile may only carry books for under fives. The public library will provide books for home reading but it will be the teachers who will be using the books with the children in school and encouraging the reading habit at home. Help by personal visits, book lists, exhibitions and courses should be regularly forthcoming from the county library concerned.

There are a few attempts to integrate a school and a public

library service, by having one library which operates as the school library in the day and the public library in the evening, at weekends, and during school holidays. Hazlewick School in West Sussex has a very attractive library; the librarian in charge is responsible for the school service and also for the children's library after the school is closed. Unlike Hazlewick, a few Leicestershire high school libraries cater for adults as well, but there is a teacher librarian responsible for service in school hours and the group librarian concerned is responsible for the branch.

There are some excellent co-operative schemes to help teachers purchase stock for their school libraries by which means they get expert help in selection and are freed from the routine work of acquisition; books arrive catalogued, fully processed and ready to go on the shelves. Hertfordshire and Wiltshire have book-selection schemes which enable schools to use their capitation grants through the county library and receive their stock on loan; through the schemes they exchange those books which they no longer require. Books bought by the schools in Leicestershire's scheme are not exchangeable as part of a school exchange unless it is considered they will be useful in other schools. Libraries send publications to their schools in which reviews appear of new titles, and which may incorporate all materials as does *Learning Resources* in Leicestershire. Teachers, education officers and librarians review books in Wiltshire's aid, *The Prospector*. Books can be ordered through these publications which may include file cards and order slips.

Exhibition collections are usually housed at headquarters where teachers can see a comprehensive range of material which has been selected as suitable for school libraries, and sometimes the reviews are included. The exhibition may be separated into material for primary schools and for secondary schools, but this will necessitate duplication and teachers, as for example a primary teacher requiring books on the history of art, may still find it necessary to look in the other collections. Adult books will also be required, particularly for the secondary schools. Exhibition collections, like that in the West Riding, range from 5,000 to 10,000 books and must be constantly revised. The exhibition collection should be housed in a place which is as accessible as possible to all areas served, so it is better to have it in the centre of the town rather than outside. Librarians should be aware, from their own experience in library suppliers, of how exhausting looking at books in large numbers is and comfort should be a primary consideration both in the planning of the shelving and of the furniture. Readily available refreshment is also an asset.

Exhibitions may also be taken out to other areas but as Sheila Ray states, there may be problems in finding somewhere to house them. Community halls are a possibility but it may be necessary to set up the exhibition each day. These exhibitions may be on specific subjects or for a certain group of people like the fifth and sixth formers. Exhibitions will also be set up to illustrate the range of books for children in colleges of education, and there may be general or specific exhibitions, for example one on music for a course for teachers of music held in the area. Books may often be ordered direct for schools from the exhibition list. Records, pictures, museum specimens, archives, films, audio and video tapes, etc. may also be included in the exhibition, particularly if there are facilities for listening and viewing. A rear projection unit would be invaluable for the automatic showing of slides of book illustrations in schools and public libraries. Films like *The Lively Art of Picture Books* from Weston Woods and the Puffin films of authors are also helpful.

Jennifer Shepherd in an article in the *Library World*, May 1967,[2] described the travelling book festivals which were organized in Shropshire during National Library Week. These were held in five rural secondary modern schools; primary schools attended from up to five miles away. In addition to displays of modern books, there was a display of old books and films on bookmaking and libraries. Attempts were made to relate books to children's interests. To entice the non-bookish child, a case of birds' eggs was put next to books on nature study, for example. In the course of a week 3,000 children living in rural areas visited these book festivals.

Exhibition vans also tour schools to enable teachers to see books and to order them on the spot. In Wiltshire one term's notice is given so that the head teachers can arrange for as many teachers as possible to see the books. Leicestershire has an extremely ambitious scheme; during the summer term the school mobiles carry selected stock for the schools to purchase themselves. The books are immediately available and are ready to be placed on the school shelves. As in Wiltshire the librarian has bibliographies to help with any book-buying queries and book lists which may also be marked up for ordering.

Loan collections to supplement a school's own stock are common in counties, county boroughs and the new Outer London boroughs. Between 1–1½ books *per capita* of children on the school roll is frequently allowed with a minimum of 100 books. In urban areas mobiles do not go to the schools and teachers are encouraged to visit headquarters and choose books from the school's collection. Transportation of the books will be arranged to the school. Sheila Ray suggests that the idea of loan collections is giving way to the provision of a completely permanent stock. She mentions in particular the secondary school with a stock of 10,000 volumes. However, there is a need for a flexible stock and books to be exchanged when no longer of use – just as branch libraries can become static and uninteresting so can the school library.

Primary schools may borrow a considerable proportion of fiction, and the exchange system is a useful opportunity for schools to try a new book before deciding whether or not to purchase it for their own stock. This is not relevant when the stock is integrated as in Wiltshire or Hertfordshire.

Teachers in the Inner London area may obtain deposit collections from County Hall. Many local libraries have built up an excellent relationship with schools, and teachers are sometimes upset when a request to borrow a deposit collection of up to 200 books is refused. It is not the function of the children's librarians of the Inner London boroughs to select books for the school library nor are the funds allocated to the children's library book funds sufficient to provide books in the libraries and the schools. The school library advisers are always extremely helpful if contacted in this situation and will visit the school concerned to see whether they can persuade the head teacher to purchase more books themselves and/or have a deposit loan from them. In practice the borough libraries are pleased to lend a few books for use in the classroom for a short period on either a range of topics or one subject, but sufficient notice should be given to get the material together. Teachers are usually issued additional tickets for the children's libraries and, like school librarians, are welcome to view on approval the books which the public library are considering for purchase.

Libraries which run a school service build up a stock of the type of material which is in demand for projects and assemble it to meet the particular requirements. A library is in difficulty if a large number of children are all working on the same subject and come in after school to borrow books. In Ontario a few years ago children from different schools often appeared to be studying the same subject at the same time. It is far easier to satisfy children if a class is working on a variety of topics.

Another problem arises in the public library when a teacher suddenly sends or comes with a group of children who want to carry on with their work by referring to relevant books. It is in this spontaneous manner, of course, that a library should be used, but it is horrifying to see the children's faces when they arrive and find there is a class already there. At times like this a study room for children is important. With overcrowding in many schools, school libraries have to be used as classrooms, which means there is not complete freedom to consult books or to take them to the classroom throughout the day. Other schools do not have a room for the library but house it in the entrance lobby or around the corridors so that the children constantly have the opportunity to see and handle books. Every classroom will also have its own collection of books. It is interesting to observe that the schools which build up their own libraries and have plenty of books in use in the classrooms, and where the teachers discuss books, are still keen supporters of the public library.

In rural areas provision is necessary particularly during the long summer holiday for children who borrow books from their schools. K. A. Stockham has described the pioneering work of Nottinghamshire County in using the school mobile.[3] Children were given bookmarks with the stops that the mobile would make printed on them, and every day there was a story hour at one of these. Kenneth Wood gives an extremely detailed account of the planning of a holiday service in Wiltshire, with the co-operation of local teachers to find out where the children live, and the finding of suitable spots to park the mobile.[4] Schools handed out tickets, to be used on the mobile, and bookmarks which gave the place and time of arrival. Story hours were not held on the route as it was felt it was necessary to reach as many children as possible. The routes were tried in advance by the adult mobiles and particular attention was paid to safety. The holiday service in Shropshire is discussed in the article previously referred to by Jennifer Shepherd, and story hours and book talks were also held.

Play centres need books, for the children to use who are in their care for the holidays. This is an excellent way of reaching children who do not normally visit the library, and librarians are welcomed, especially for story-telling. Courses have also been held training play leaders in story-telling at public libraries, particularly in North America. It is necessary to stress that the library wishes the books borrowed to be used, and that children should be allowed to take home the books that they are enjoying. Lambeth has also organized stories in parks during the holidays.

Holidays become a problem in urban areas where mothers work, and children need the companionship of an adult whom they feel cares for them as well as the society of other children. There are frequently insufficient play areas, particularly in bad weather, and many of the play centres run by voluntary organizations other than the Education Authority rely on student help and are only open in the summer. Libraries organize activities such as story hours, book and music programmes, story and painting sessions, the production of a library magazine, craftwork like the making of mobiles to display in the libraries and puppetry, but few of our libraries are so well staffed that they can meet the needs of the children who come in to choose books and seek information, as well as those of the children who are there continuously. An activity room would be useful and adequate staff are necessary to organize all this.

Whether or not the authority is responsible for the service to schools, there should be close liaison between the local library and its schools. Teachers should be encouraged to bring their classes to the library but it is best if the librarian goes to the school first to discuss the library service with the head teacher and talk to the teachers and children in the classrooms. Application cards can be left with the school and when completed they can be sent to the library so that when the class visits the children's tickets are ready. Classes may make a single visit for an introduction to the library or perhaps three or four visits to allow the children to get used to the routine of taking out and returning books. A class may come for a term or a year and the visits may be at weekly, fortnightly or monthly intervals. The librarian must not allow her enthusiasm to run away with her; taking classes is exhausting and it is important that the librarian is still capable of giving her best to the children who come on their own after school. A keen school should not be allowed unintentionally to monopolize the time-table; the library should be equally available to all schools in its catchment area. It is better to welcome every class for an occasional visit and to suggest that at some stage in their school career they should come regularly to the library for book talks. But if children attend for book talks during all their primary school years they may tend to associate the library with a school time-table and not see it as a place they can use at their leisure.

For the introductory visits, tickets should be made out and ready for any children who do not already belong to the library so that they can borrow books immediately if desired. A display of books is usually set up which is appropriate to the age and interests of the children. The librarian will give a short talk on the library service, about books to take home to read and reference books which must be used in the library. She will tell the children about books which may be referred to or borrowed on a variety of subjects such as bird identification, how to make a kite, pets and how to look after them, history, poetry and stamp catalogues. The library may lend pictures and gramophone records and the librarian will also tell them about any events in the library, for example story hours or library clubs. Older children in primary schools should be given some idea of how books are arranged on the shelves and told that the number on the spine is a symbol representing a subject so that books on the same or related subjects are placed together on the shelves. Children should also be shown the subject index so that they can find the class number for different subjects. Some libraries make a game out of this and give the children cards with different subjects on so that they can find the number and then the books on the shelves. In general the use of catalogues is better left until the need arises and the librarian can show the

4

child concerned individually. Finding information from books is important and this can be covered in a school class with children being shown how to use a contents list and an index. The range of reference books and the type of questions which they will answer should be demonstrated, but it is important that children should understand that books which are available for home reading will also help them with their homework. The librarian will be pleased to welcome them if they wish to do their homework in the library and will help them to find any information they may need.

When classes visit the library regularly book talks are given to introduce worthwhile books which it is felt they will enjoy but might miss. Methods of giving book talks vary, sometimes one book may be discussed, on other occasions three or four, or perhaps a dozen. A theme may be chosen which includes both fiction and non-fiction like animals, time, space travel or history and perhaps covering a full range of materials like Jackdaws, records and films. A poem can also be used as part of a theme, or the whole talk can be on poetry, or the class can be invited to hear a group like 'The Around Readers' giving a poetry reading. It is usual to read from one or more of the books in a book talk to give the children a flavour of the author's style and perhaps stop where a climax has been reached. Themes have the advantage that books can be included to cover many reading abilities. Librarians are sometimes afraid to use myths and legends with children, yet here are some of the most exciting stories ever written, which appeal to both boys and girls, available at different levels. There is an extremely useful introduction to myths and legends which studies the books available and their use with children called *The Ordinary and the Fabulous* by Elizabeth Cook.[5] Story-telling is also a valuable aid and is covered in Chapter 8.

Teachers and librarians are becoming far more aware of the work each is doing in schools and libraries, and are giving and receiving help and advice from each other. Joint conferences have been organized at Homerton College, Cambridge, with emphasis on the school library service by the Department of Education and Science, and short courses on literature were held at Exeter University.

The School Library Association was formed in 1937. Membership includes teachers, librarians and institutions. It publishes the *School Librarian* four times a year which is extremely valuable as a reviewing media, apart from excellent articles on school libraries and using books in schools. The Teacher/Librarian Certificate is sponsored by the School Library Association and the Library Association. Teachers must have had three years' experience before sitting the exam, and courses are organized by some local authorities.

There is also a School Library Association Annual Conference which is attended by both teachers and librarians, advisers and inspectors. Useful book lists are published by both the School Library Association in Scotland and the School Library Association. Some local authorities run courses on the school library and books as part of an in-service training scheme. Courses on children's literature and the use of books in schools are being run in colleges of education. It is encouraging to find that students are studying libraries as their special subject and are asking to spend a week or two in a public library during their holidays to use books with children and see the services the library offers. Colleges of education are also sending groups of students to public libraries for talks about books and discussion on the reception of classes from schools, and other activities.

Wiltshire County Library contributes to the induction programme of new teachers and makes them immediately aware of the services offered by the County Library. Birmingham has an interesting scheme of co-operation between school and library services by the formation of area links as described by Ronald E. Crook in the *Library Association Record*, March 1970.[6]

The building up of resource centres in education is a challenge in librarianship today. The Library Association recommended standards for use in schools in 1970 and 1972[7], and issued relevant policy statements in 1971[8] and 1973[9].

The Knapp School Library Projects as described in *Impact*[10] and *Realization*[11] were a demonstration project financed by the Knapp Foundation to bring selected schools up to the *National Standards for School Libraries* (United States), and to show the educational value of highly developed school libraries to students and teachers, educationalists and local authorities.

The direct involvement of the teaching faculties at the universities was of particular value, as lecturers and students had the opportunity to see the assistance which could be given in teaching by a well-developed school library.

The visiting programme demonstrated the value of a school library, and resulted in considerable improvement in school libraries in many parts of the country.

In Britain the deliberations of the Library Association School Libraries' Committee on School Standards were well received; it would be of value in Britain to demonstrate in selected schools throughout the country the educational value of a developed and efficient library service based on these standards.

REFERENCES

1 Sheila Ray. *The Library Service to Schools*. Library Association Pamphlet no. 32. London, Library Association, 2nd ed. 1972.

2 Jennifer Shepherd. 'Working with Children in a Rural Library'. *Library World*, vol. 68, no. 803, May 1967. pp. 302–4.

3 K. A. Stockham. 'The Holiday Mobile'. *Books*, March 1962. p. 63.

4 Kenneth Wood. 'Books for Holidays: A Mobile Service for Children in Rural Wiltshire'. *Library World*, vol. 69, no. 811, 1968. pp. 170–1.

5 Elizabeth Cook. *The Ordinary and the Fabulous: An Introduction to Myths, Legends and Fairy Tales for Teachers and Storytellers*. London, Cambridge University Press, 1969.

6 Ronald E. Crook. 'Kingstanding Schools and Library Link'. *Library Association Record*, vol. 72, no. 8, March 1970. pp. 106–7.

7 *School Library Resource Centres: Recommended Standards for Policy and Provision*. London, Library Association, 1970. *Supplement on Non-Book Materials*, London, Library Association, 1972.

8 Library Association. *A Policy Statement on School Library Resource Centres*. London, Library Association, 1971.

9 Library Association. 'Library Resource Centres in Schools, Colleges and Institutions of Higher Education: A General Policy Statement'. *Library Association Record*, vol. 75, March 1973. p. 52.

10 *Impact: the School Library and the Instructional Program. A Report on Phase 1 of the Knapp School Libraries Project* by Peggy Sullivan. Chicago, American Library Association, 1967.

11 *Realization: the Final Report of the Knapp School Libraries Project* edited by Peggy Sullivan. Chicago, American Library Association, *c.* 1968.

FURTHER READING

Blandford, Shirley. 'The Role of the Professional Librarian in the School'. *Library Association Record*, vol. 71, no. 7, July 1969. pp. 207–9.
Edwards, R. P. A. 'The Resource Centre in a Flexible School'. *Library Association Record*, vol. 71, no. 8, August 1969. pp. 237–40.
Schools Council. *School Resource Centres*. London, Evans/Methuen, 1972.
Shepherd, Jennifer. 'The Library Service in Schools in the Seventies'. *Proceedings of the Public Libraries Conference. Held at Eastbourne, 1970*. London, Library Association, 1970.

Chapter 8
Story-telling

To be able to create a story, to make it live during the moment of the telling, to arouse emotions – wonder, laughter, joy, amazement – this is the only goal a storyteller may have.

From The Way of the Storyteller by RUTH SAWYER[1]

Today story-telling is still a natural and essential art in many parts of the world, but is it really necessary in an advanced, technological and literate society? Have we not got other media – television, radio and tape-recorders – that we could use to better advantage, or why not allow the child to read the book or story for himself? Children will receive pleasure and derive benefit from reading a folk or hero story. However, these tales come to us from an oral tradition, and this ideally is how they should be introduced. The story-teller who has lived with the story for weeks, months or even years will have spent considerable time on the preparation, by comparing versions, and have prepared the telling carefully. It should evolve into a story which is alive to the children present. Through a brief introduction, if necessary, she will have placed them in the period and mood of the tale. She will be able to bring the characters to life, and will, to a certain extent, adjust the telling of her story by watching the reaction on the children's faces. Some audiences will immediately see the humour in a story like *Lazy Jack* or *Goose Hans*, and will laugh in anticipation. With other children it is necessary to pause so that they can catch up with the humour. When one child is frightened by an episode which the others are enjoying, the story-teller can catch that child's eye and reassure him, without spoiling the effect for the rest. Before telling a story, while getting her own breath and relaxing for a few seconds, she will quickly sum up her audience from the point of view of their age, mood and experience, to decide whether the story she had prepared would be better left to another time. The inexperienced story-teller will have more difficulty here until she has a small repertoire to draw on. Even with a weekly story hour, the child will only hear a small proportion of the legends, folk tales and hero stories which we hope he will read. However, if by listening to stories well told, his imagination has been stimulated, it will be easier to visualize and experience the events when he is reading himself. I am not suggesting here that story-telling is merely a means to encourage further reading. It is a valid art in its own right, and the purpose is to create a story at the time of telling.

The disadvantage of radio and gramophone records is the physical absence of the story-teller. The story may be beautifully told, possibly with sound effects, but the presence of the story-teller is missing. It is a two-way process; the story-teller watches the reaction of the children, the children are drawn towards her and look at her face, her eyes, and the movement of her hands and head. When recordings are used the volume of sound can be altered but not the pace of the story to meet the needs of a particular audience at a particular time. Disastrously I once used a gramophone record of *Rapunzel* which is beautifully told by Joseph Schildkraut. Possibly it was his accent (which enhances the story for adults) and the fact that many of the children's native language was not English, perhaps it was a fraction too fast for them to hear and comprehend all the words, but the children became fidgety and it was a frustrating experience. But the great advantage of radio and gramophone records is that the child still has his own visual experience. Many adults today remember *Children's Hour* as one of the delights of childhood.

Television dramatizes books and stories and often has done this so well that interest in extremely worthwhile books has been revived. Picture books are used on *Play School*, and there has been some excellent straight story-telling with a minimum of illustration allowing the children to visualize the action in *Jackanory*. Here the children can see the story-teller, but again the pace cannot be altered to suit the audience, and the story-teller misses the stimulation and response from a group of children. Some years ago on a Sunday programme David Kossoff told stories from the Bible with a small group of children present, which was most attractive. As an experiment Westminster installed a television set in one of the children's libraries to see if the children would like to watch *Jackanory* and other suitable programmes, but it was not successful and has been abandoned.

A busy library may have several weekly periods set aside for story-telling. The programme for under fives will be during the day when the older children are at school. If it is during the afternoon, it must finish early enough for the mothers to fetch their other children from school. A story hour may be held on Saturday mornings to attract children between five and eight. Traditionally we speak of the story hour, but in some libraries the period can be half an hour, and it may be about ten minutes to a quarter of an hour for very young children.

Children who attend story time for the under fives are usually brought by their mothers, or in small groups from day nurseries or playgroups. To interest the mothers who already bring children to the library to change books, a poster is displayed to advertise it, and to ask the mothers to give their child's name to the librarian if they wish to bring him. The librarian will then, if necessary, get to know the child before he comes and will have some idea of how many children to expect. The Maternity and Child Welfare Clinics are normally very glad to advertise the library service, but there is a risk of being swamped with small children and their mothers, particularly in suburban areas. The ideal number is between six and twelve children – once fifteen is reached it is worth considering holding two sessions. Librarians who give talks to clubs for mothers and other organizations have the opportunity to suggest taking small children to the library to choose books and listen to stories. It is usually necessary for day nurseries and playgroups to have their own period because of the numbers of children.

If the library is open plan and does not have a separate activities room or area which can be partitioned off, it must be made clear to all users when it is the younger children's special period of the week. Adults should not be unnecessarily concerned over a reasonable amount of noise and high spirits. A notice prominently displayed will serve as a reminder to readers if they wish to avoid this time. In areas where many children wish to attend, it may be necessary to hold special sessions lasting about six to eight weeks to give everyone the opportunity of coming. The advantage of this is that all the children are new together which is easier when selecting stories. On the other hand, with one or two new children, it is easier to give them special attention (but unobtrusively) both during the story time and when they are choosing books afterwards.

Picture books are largely used for story-telling with little children. *Wake Up Farm* by Alvin Tresselt is an excellent introduction. The children enjoy making the noises of the animals and chanting 'Wake up farm'. *The Pirate Twins* by William Nicholson is a simple story of a little girl, Mary, who found the twins on a beach in Jamaica, and bathed, fed and tried to teach them. It has a very simple text, gentle humour and expressive pictures which completely tell the story. The *Harry* series by Gene Zion are invariably enjoyed by small children who also identify themselves with such favourites as Angus in *Angus and the Ducks* by Marjorie Flack. Other books which have been particularly successful are *Mr Gumpy's Outing* and *Humbert* by John Burningham, *Whistle for Willie* by Ezra Keats, *My Hopping Bunny* by Robert Bright, *The Rain Puddle* by Adelaide Holl, *Mike Mulligan and His Steam Shovel* by Virginia Lee Burton, and *Rosie's Walk* by Pat Hutchins.

Picture books should be held open towards the children so that they can follow the events through the pictures. When there is a single line of text it is possible to read sideways, otherwise the tale will have to be told in the story-teller's own words or learnt by heart first – either method requires careful preparation – and it is necessary to ensure that the pictures correspond exactly with the part of the story being told. It is a good idea to start the session with a finger play or nursery rhyme, so that late arrivals do not miss or spoil part of the story for others. *Lavender's Blue*, compiled by Kathleen Lines and illustrated by Harold Jones, and *This Little Pig Went to Market*, compiled by Norah Montgomerie and illustrated by Margery Gill, are invaluable both for ideas for actions in story time and more intimately at home. There are also some beautiful nursery rhyme books, such as *The Mother Goose Treasury* by Raymond Briggs and *The White Land* and *Ring a Ring O' Roses*.

It is a good idea to have one or two nursery rhymes after the story for the children to chant and act. A less familiar one can be included so that the children will learn a few new ones. Miss Jarecki, who is an adviser on the training of playgroup leaders in Inner London, felt that only one story should be told and then repeated, as one story is enough for young children to take in at a time.

However, there are children who have been in the habit of listening to stories, both at home and at the library, for a considerable time. These children ask for a second story, and if the story-teller has not got one ready they quickly produce a book which is usually difficult or unsuitable to tell or read from. It is better to encourage the newer children and the younger ones to go to their mothers and choose their books while telling another story to the nucleus left. The children concerned have enjoyed simple repetitive tales like *Johnny Cake*, *The Three Billy-Goats Gruff*, *The Story of the Three Bears* or *The Three Little Pigs*. The last two stories may be told in two parts, finishing the first part of *The Story of the Three Bears* when Goldilocks goes to sleep, and the first part of *The Three Little Pigs* when the third little pig has built his house of bricks. Other useful sources of stories to tell are Eileen Colwell's *The Youngest Storybook* which has good advice on the technique[2] and a few of the stories from *The Faber Story Book* edited by Kathleen Lines, although many of them are more suitable for telling to older children.

Picture books with slightly more sophisticated ideas are *May I Bring a Friend?* by Beatrice Schenk de Regniers and Beni Montresor, *The Three Robbers* by Tomi Ungerer, *The Rich Man and the Shoemaker* and other fables of La Fontaine, illustrated by Brian Wildsmith, and *The Tale of Peter Rabbit* by Beatrix Potter.

Librarians differ on whether it is better to have the parent in the room with the child or not. In some libraries the mother may leave the child and go shopping for a short period. Others prefer to have the parent if not in the room, then in the library. At East York Library, a township outside Toronto, a pre-school story hour was held during the summer before the children attended the kindergarten class in school. The children used to arrive specially dressed for the occasion; the mothers regarded it as a social gathering and asked to see short films on child psychology which would help them to bring up their children, and also held discussion groups. A librarian who encourages the mother to leave the child has said that there is never any difficulty as long as she returns by the end of story time, which lasts about half an hour.

Joan E. Cass in her book *Literature and the Young Child* discusses books to introduce to young children.[3] She emphasizes that they need stories about things and people they are familiar with, and that stories of magic, the supernatural or folk tales where parents abandon children or have cruel stepmothers are best avoided. Books, however, about toys that come to life are acceptable as the child believes his toys have a life of their own and are capable of feelings. 'Stories in which animals or machines are captured, tamed or managed by the child, dominated by him or their roles taken over, have a very strong appeal, both to the under-fives and to the five and eight year old.' Marie Shedlock in her book *The Art of the Story-teller*[4] discussed *The Constant Tin Soldier* by Hans Christian Andersen as it followed the pattern of development which young children require from their stories. First they want familiar events and familiar objects, then unusual happenings to a familiar object in a place known to them, e.g. toys coming to life, and finally the completely unusual happening outside the home, when adventures like those of the little tin soldier will stretch their imagination and experience.

Apart from the story hours or story times, classes of young children can be told stories during library visits. Often picture books are used – with the infants' classes most of the books already mentioned are popular. *Crictor* by Tomi Ungerer is enjoyed particularly when children are learning letters and numbers, so is poor *Petunia*, the creation of Roger Duvoisin, who carried a book around because she wanted to be clever. Wanda Gag's *Millions of Cats*, *The Tale of Johnny Town Mouse* by Beatrix Potter, *The Story of Horace* by Alice M. Coats, and *Where the Wild Things Are* by Maurice Sendak are excellent for bridging the gap between the simple picture books and the telling of folk and fairy stories. It is a good idea sometimes to have a straight telling of a story like *Molly Whuppie* and *Rapunzel*, and on other occasions to use a picture book.

In the story hour the ages may range from five to eleven or even under fives may come. It is more satisfactory to tell a story to the youngest first either using a picture book or a repetitive tale, and then to allow those who have had enough to go, and tell the main story to the rest. It is advisable to have another member of staff on duty apart from the story-teller to talk to the children and to help them select books. Some libraries have a story hour for the under nines on Saturdays, and a club for the over nines during the week. This definitely helps in the selection of material and gives more scope for the older children. The Library Club can include other activities such as writing plays and acting, play reading, book discussions and talks by staff and visiting lecturers. Story-telling, although more difficult with a mixed age range, is a stimulating and rewarding experience.

Marie Shedlock's book *The Art of the Story-teller* is invaluable to all story-tellers, whether novices or experienced. It is essentially a practical book which illustrates through Marie Shedlock's own experience how to select stories; how to tell them; and the difficulties which may arise. Ruth Sawyer described the impact of Marie Shedlock when she first heard her thus: 'She might have been the Danish fairy man himself, telling his own stories for the first time to a group of children. The words were Andersen's but so were they Miss Shedlock's; the story might have been a figment of her imagination made manifest. . . . Here was an art whose seeming simplicity and directness only hid for a novice the difficulties of its accomplishment.' This quotation is from *The Way of the Storyteller*, which also gives excellent practical advice on the preparation and telling of stories.

Folk and fairy stories, Bible stories, hero tales, short stories or parts of books are excellent and suitable material. For the beginner, the folk and fairy stories are probably the most successful and the cumulative and repetitive tales, like *The Old Woman and Her Pig* and *The Gingerbread Man* are the easiest for a beginner to learn.

Folk stories are dramatic; events tend to follow a pattern; things happen in threes, or the youngest child who is considered stupid triumphs over his more favoured siblings. The children and the teller can readily visualize the development of the plot, and the stories have immediate appeal, if well told, to the majority of children. The story is a complete experience in itself, unlike a book talk in which the aim is to whet the appetite and persuade the children to read.

Every library system should build up a collection of books for use in story-telling, and each librarian should have readily available books to use herself, and to use in advising others about possible sources of material. Some of us are grateful for the care which has been taken by some libraries to preserve old collections such as Steel's *English Fairy Tales*, which is now out of print in this country. Particular care must be taken when withdrawing collections that sufficient copies of valuable books are kept on restricted access in case they go out of print in the future.

At Boys' and Girls' House in Toronto, a staff training course was held on story-telling. One group consisted of staff from as far away as Australia, Turkey, Hungary, Trinidad, England and different parts of Canada. With unending patience and tact, the librarian in charge gave advice on how to select stories; which stories would be most suitable for beginners; which, in the case of different nationalities, personalities, voices and accents, would suit the individual story-teller. The selected stories were learnt by heart, and told to the other members of the groups. Help was given here on how to present the story and how to hold the attention of the audience. The librarian gave advice on any problems of voice production, pronunciation, and how to use any natural characteristics, e.g. spontaneous movement of the hands or accents, to the maximum effect. A cumulative story was learnt first and then a progression was made to the full range of folk and fairy stories, frequently choosing stories of the tellers' countries. Finally a cycle of *Dragon Stories* was held, for which the participants visited different libraries in the city for the Saturday morning story hour. Most participants were beginners, and were initially appalled at the idea of telling stories to each other, but through listening to others and hearing their comments on each other's story new ideas evolved and also sufficient confidence to enjoy storytelling with children. To go to other libraries was a particularly useful experience, as the audiences in different parts of the city, being of different national and cultural backgrounds, responded in their own way to the stories. A second course succeeded this on myths, legends and hero stories. In a scholarly manner the librarian described basic texts of the Icelandic sagas, from which arose different versions suitable for children, and compared them. We all took a particular topic, e.g. Beowulf, Roland, King Arthur, and Irish, Welsh or Greek legends, and gave a talk describing the adventures and characters and comparing different sources and versions for content and method of presentation. I think several members wished they had heard more of the hero stories in their own childhood.

The beginner will need to explore many collections of tales until she finds something that she enjoys and would like to share with others. She will probably need to read the story several times. Then other versions of the same story should be read to see which to base her telling on and whether there are any particular features she wishes to include from others. Story-tellers, like students, vary in the methods they use to learn their stories. It is best to read the story through several times at intervals, then just think about it, allowing the actions and characters to take over, and to visualize it in your own imagination. The next step is to write down the essentials of the plot from memory (some people prefer to learn a story in parts and finally bring the sections together). Re-read the text or texts and compare them with the notes making any necessary alterations. The next step is to tell the story aloud listening to the sound of the words, and deciding whether or not they are suitable and in keeping with the story. A tape-recorder is invaluable for this purpose. When re-telling stories great care must be taken that the selection of words is appropriate to the period, setting and atmosphere of the original. Finally, re-read the text again and make a note and learn by heart any rhythmic or descriptive features which enhance the telling. There are arguments about whether stories should be learned word by word, or whether they should be told in the teller's own words. Ruth Sawyer felt only story-tellers of the calibre of Marie Shedlock and Anna Cogswell Taylor could tell stories memorized word by word from the text, and really spontaneously re-create the story. Marie Shedlock said: 'If the style is classic or if the interest of the story is closely connected with the style, as in Andersen, Kipling or Stevenson, then it is better to commit it absolutely to memory.' She considered both methods were necessary for the story-teller. When memorizing stories word by word from the text it is essential to allow the plot, characters and inter-relationships to develop in the same way as when telling the story in one's own words. It is impossible to tell a story convincingly and portray the varying characters and illustrate dramatic changes in the plot unless the story is alive in the imagination. Once it is the text must be read and re-read and the pictures it creates in the mind must be visualized. Any unnecessary parts to the action of the story may be omitted. Some people find learning by heart easier than others. Once learnt the story needs to be compared with the text by writing it down, tape-recording it, or telling it aloud. It is necessary to time every story to know how long it will last when considering content for a story-telling programme or class.

Stories need an immediate introduction inherent in the actual beginning of the story which will place the child's mind in the right time and place. It is essential that anything which is necessary to the understanding of the story be discussed at the beginning, not in the middle of a story when the attention of the children and the continuity of the story will be interrupted. An example of a good introduction which immediately places the listener in the story is 'Once upon a time, a long while ago, when all the world was young and all sorts of strange things happened', from 'Caporushes' in *Tales of Magic and Enchantment* chosen and edited by Kathleen Lines. This beginning allays a child's fears by placing him in a land of make-believe and not in his daily life, as discussed by Tolkien in *Tree and Leaf*.[5]

Whether the story is true is not so important as whether the events could happen to children now. One is given an immediate picture of the terrifying strength of Cucullen in the words : 'Some giants are stronger than others, and of all the giants that ever lived in Ireland, the giant Cucullen was the strongest.' (From 'Finn MacCool and Cucullen' in *A Book of Giants* by Ruth Manning-Sanders.) And here is a picture of a greedy little boy : 'Once upon a time there was an old wife who sat and baked. Now you must know that this old wife had a little son who was so plump and fat, and so fond of good things that they called him Buttercup; she had a dog too, whose name was Goldtooth.' (From 'Buttercup' in *Popular Tales from the Norse* by Asbjörnsen and Moe.)

A good ending is extremely important. The story-teller should have gradually released the tension and excitement letting the children down gently. Some endings are snappy, others end in a question and the children have to imagine what happened, and others have the traditional 'living happily ever after'. The Norwegian folktales often have excellent endings like 'Snip, snip, snover, this story's over !' (From 'Kate Woodencloak' in

Popular Tales from the Norse by Asbjörnsen and Moe.) A contrast
comes from 'The Giant Who Had No Heart in His Body' : 'So he
sent out and called a great wedding feast, and the mirth was
both loud and long, and if they have not done feasting, why
they are still at it.' The ending of 'Finn MacCool and Cucullen'
leaves the listener wondering : 'But where he fled to no one can
tell. He was never more seen in those parts.'

Ruth Sawyer compares the stories you tell with the clothes
you wear; some suit you, some do not. It may be necessary to
abandon a story even after a considerable amount of work if the
teller is not happy about its development and her portrayal of
it. This happens, too, when a story-teller, on meeting the
audience, feels that the story or stories she has prepared to tell
are unsuitable for this particular group of children, possibly
because of their ages or the present mood of the children. If she
has a varied repertoire, the experienced story-teller will quickly
sum up her audience and tell something more appropriate for
the particular group present. Ruth Sawyer suggested having
a laboratory group of children well used to stories to try out new
ones on. It is also possible to experiment with stories, if school
classes regularly visit the library, but different groups should be
used so that one or two classes are not always the guinea pigs.
This gives one a good idea of their response to the telling, but
unless it is a family-grouped class, only one age is present and it
is not so difficult as with mixed ages at the story hour; the latter
is more stimulating and often extremely rewarding.

Marie Shedlock discussed the problem of story-telling thus:
'The art of telling stories is, in truth, much more difficult than
acting a part on the stage. First, because the narrator is responsible for the whole drama and the whole atmosphere which
surrounds it. He has to live the life of each character and understand the relation which each bears to the whole. Secondly,
because the stage is a miniature one, gestures and movements
must all be so adjusted as not to destroy the sense of proportion.'
This sums up the way a story-teller should train herself to tell
stories, not as an actress portraying a part, however brilliantly,
but far more intimately re-creating a story which is complete
in itself, acting as the narrator as well as each of the characters.
She is responsible for building up anticipation and suspense
and allowing the audience to relax but not completely, so that

they are ready for further action in the plot. In the theatre there are sound effects and use of lighting, and in films the inevitable background music to convey atmosphere. Marie Shedlock's second point is that the stage for a story-teller is miniature; she should sit or stand with her audience closely grouped around her. It would be a good idea for anyone using gestures to watch herself tell a story in front of a full-length mirror. So often, unless they are extremely subtle, gestures can draw attention to the story-teller herself instead of the story she is telling, and the sequence of the tale can be lost in the listeners' minds. Spontaneous movements of the hands can be attractive as, naturally, we talk with our hands as well as our voices. A gift of mimicry is an asset when portraying animals and people, but characters should not be overdramatized, or the balance of the tale can be lost. Every telling of a story will be different; by watching the faces of the listening children and seeing their reaction to the humour of the story, the story-teller will modify the speed and weight of her voice and pause for effect, so that their attention is held and they receive the maximum pleasure.

Certainly poetry has a valid place in a story hour. David McCord has written that he regrets that children are not read aloud to in their homes today, and that they are out of touch with natural elements.[6] Through reading aloud children gain an instinctive feeling for rhythm and the sounds of words. Poetry may be chosen for sheer beauty, like Walter De La Mare's work, or, as a contrast to a long story, a humorous poem may be chosen, for instance Edward Lear's 'The Quangle Wangles' Hat', or 'The King's Breakfast' by A. A. Milne. Selections from Ian Serrailler's adaptation of ballads, and 'The Pied Piper of Hamelin' by Robert Browning, are good material for the main feature. A picture book or a short story may be included as well.

Story and painting sessions are held in some libraries particularly during the holidays. Frequently, in areas where the children spend large portions of their time in the library, the main purpose is to keep the children occupied. Marie Shedlock felt it was a mistake to ask children to repeat a story after it had been told, and that the illustration of the story, although interesting, should be used very sparingly. A main problem is that the time lag between the story and the painting is too short.

Ruth Sawyer told stories in prisons, missions, hospitals, camps, and in women's and university clubs. As Tolkien in *Tree and Leaf* wrote, fairy stories and folklore are not especially intended for children, and it is largely because of the verbal tradition of the stories that nurses told them to their charges. Appreciation of these stories may well increase with age. In 1920 a headmistress of a London school suggested the revival of the bard of former times as a professional member of the staff in libraries.[7] She suggested that children should be brought from local schools to listen to ballads and stories, and that opportunities should also be made for evening sessions for adults and for children who had left school. Today surely such an idea would be well received in homes and clubs for the elderly, the blind and physically handicapped people, especially where there are mechanical or visual problems in the reading of books.

REFERENCES

1 Ruth Sawyer. *The Way of the Storyteller.* New edition. London, The Bodley Head, 1966.

2 Eileen Colwell. *The Youngest Storybook.* London, The Bodley Head, 1967.

3 Joan E. Cass. *Literature and the Young Child.* Education Today. London, Longmans, 1967.

4 Marie L. Shedlock. *The Art of the Story-teller.* London, Constable, 1915, reprinted 1951.

5 J. R. R. Tolkien. *Tree and Leaf.* London, Allen and Unwin, 1964.

6 David McCord. 'Poetry for Children' in *A Critical Approach to Children's Literature,* edited by Sara Innis Fenwick. Chicago, University of Chicago Press, 1967.

7 Mrs A. M. Frayer. 'Co-operation between Public Libraries and Elementary Schools'. *Library Association Record,* vol. 22, 1920. pp. 64–70.

STORIES TO TELL

Andersen, Hans Christian. *Fairy Tales and Legends.* Illustrated by Rex Whistler. New edition includes 'The Constant Tin Soldier'. London, The Bodley Head, 1959.

Asbjörnsen, Peter Christen, and Jörgen I. Moe. *Popular Tales from the Norse.* Includes 'Buttercup', 'The Giant Who Had No Heart in His Body', 'Katie Woodencloak', and 'The Three Billy-Goats Gruff'. London, The Bodley Head, 1969.

Briggs, Raymond. *The Mother Goose Treasury*. London, Hamish Hamilton, 1966.

Briggs, Raymond. *Ring A Ring O' Roses*. London, Hamish Hamilton, 1962.

Briggs, Raymond. *The White Land*. London, Hamish Hamilton, 1963.

Bright, Robert. *My Hopping Bunny*. Tadworth, World's Work, 1967.

Browning, Robert. *The Pied Piper of Hamelin*. Illustrated by Alan Howard. London, Faber, 1967.

Burningham, John. *Humbert*. London, Cape, 1965.

Burningham, John. *Mr. Gumpy's Outing*. London, Cape, 1970.

Burton, Virginia Lee. *Mike Mulligan and His Steam Shovel*. London, Faber, 1966.

'Buttercup'. *See under* Peter Christen Asbjörnsen and Jörgen I. Moe above.

'Caporushes'. *See under* Kathleen Lines below.

Coats, Alice M. *The Story of Horace*. London, Faber, 1937.

Colwell, Eileen. *The Younger Story Book*. London, The Bodley Head, 1967.

'The Constant Tin Soldier'. *See under* Hans Christian Andersen above.

Duvoisin, Roger. *Petunia*. London, The Bodley Head, 1958.

'Finn MacCool and Cucullen'. *See under* Ruth Manning-Sanders below.

Flack, Marjorie. *Angus and the Ducks*. London, The Bodley Head, 1970.

Gag, Wanda. *Millions of Cats*. London, Faber, 1929.

'The Giant Who Had No Heart in His Body'. *See under* Peter Christen Asbjörnsen and Jörgen I. Moe above.

'The Gingerbread Man'. *See under* Barbara Ireson below.

'Goose Hans'. *See under* J. L. and W. K. Grimm below.

Grimm, J. L. and W. K. *Household Stories*. Translated from the German and illustrated by Lucy Crane. Includes 'Rapunzel'. London, Constable, n.d.

Grimm, J. L. and W. K. *Three Gay Tales from Grimm*. Freely translated and illustrated by Wanda Gag. Includes 'Goose Hans'. London, Faber, 1962.

Holl, Adelaide. *The Rain Puddle*. London, The Bodley Head, 1966.

Hutchins, Pat. *Rosie's Walk*. London, The Bodley Head, 1968.

Ireson, Barbara. *The Gingerbread Man*. Includes 'The Gingerbread Man', 'Lazy Jack', 'The Old Woman and Her Pig', 'The Story of the Three Bears', 'The Story of the Three Little Pigs'. London, Muller, 1942.

Jacobs, Joseph. *English Fairy Tales*. Includes 'Johnny Cake', 'Lazy Jack', 'The Old Woman and Her Pig', 'The Story of the Three Bears', 'The Story of the Three Little Pigs'. London, Muller, 1942.

'Johnny Cake'. *See under* Joseph Jacobs above.

'Katie Woodencloak'. *See under* Peter Christen Asbjörnsen and Jörgen I. Moe above.

Keats, Ezra. *Whistle for Willie*. London, The Bodley Head, 1966.

'The King's Breakfast'. *See under* A. A. Milne below.

La Fontaine, Jean de. *The Rich Man and the Shoemaker*. Illustrated by Brian Wildsmith. London, Oxford University Press, 1965.

'Lazy Jack'. *See under* Joseph Jacobs above.

Lear, Edward. *The Quangle Wangles' Hat*. Pictures by Helen Oxenbury. London, Heinemann, 1969.

Lines, Kathleen (ed.). *The Faber Storybook*. London, Faber, 1961.

Lines, Kathleen. *Lavender's Blue*. London, Oxford University Press, 1959.

Lines, Kathleen. *Tales of Magic and Enchantment*. Includes 'Caporushes'. London, Faber, 1966.

Manning-Sanders, Ruth. *A Book of Giants*. Includes 'Finn MacCool and Cucullen'. London, Methuen, 1962.

Mare, Walter De La. *Tales Told Again*. Includes 'Mollie Whuppie'. London, Faber, 1959.

Milne, A. A. *The World of Christopher Robin*. Illustrated by E. H. Shepard. Includes 'The King's Breakfast'. London, Methuen, 1924.

'Molly Whuppie'. *See under* Walter De La Mare above.

Montgomerie, Norah. *This Little Pig Went to Market*. London, The Bodley Head, 1966.

Nicholson, William. *The Pirate Twins*. London, Faber, 1929.

'The Old Woman and Her Pig'. *See under* Joseph Jacobs above.

Potter, Beatrix. *The Tale of Johnny Town Mouse*. London, Warne, 1918.

Potter, Beatrix. *The Tale of Peter Rabbit*. London, Warne, 1902.

'Rapunzel'. *See under* J. L. and W. K. Grimm above.

Schenk de Regniers, Beatrice, and Beni Montresor. *May I Bring a Friend?* London, Collins, 1966.

Sendak, Maurice. *Where the Wild Things Are*. London, The Bodley Head, 1967.

Steel, Flora Annie. *English Fairy Tales*. Illustrated by Arthur Rackham. London, Macmillan, 1918.

'The Story of the Three Bears'. *See under* Joseph Jacobs above.

'The Story of the Three Little Pigs'. *See under* Joseph Jacobs above.

'The Three Billy-Goats Gruff'. *See under* Peter Christen Asbjörnsen and Jörgen I. Moe above.

Tresselt, Alvin. *Wake Up Farm*. Tadworth, World's Work, 1966.

Ungerer, Tomi. *Crictor*. London, Methuen, 1959.

Ungerer, Tomi. *The Three Robbers*. London, Methuen, 1964.

Zion, Gene. *Harry the Dirty Dog*. Pictures by Margaret Bloy Graham. London, The Bodley Head, 1956.

Chapter 9
Other Activities in Libraries

The purpose of activities in libraries is to open up new horizons for the child, covering a wide range of knowledge, especially the kind that children may not have the opportunity to develop in their homes or for themselves. If one considers the library as a cultural centre, the term 'extension activities' is unfortunate as, given the right facilities, staffing and finance, they are an inherent part of the work of the library.

Activities in libraries are a good idea provided they are not a gimmicky window dressing without the backing of a good stock and suitably trained staff to work with the children. The organization of events is extremely time-consuming and senior children's librarians should assess whether or not an undue proportion of their time is being spent on this in relation to more important work such as book selection, stock revision, school visiting and staff training.

Some authorities have a sum in the estimates for extension work, others have little or no specific finance. In some authorities the decision as to which speakers to invite is left to the children's librarian concerned, in others proposals may have to go to the committee. It is often more worthwhile and less time-consuming to have fewer events but to use the best professionals and to concentrate on larger audiences if there is the necessary/ space to make this viable. On the other hand it may be preferable to have activities that children can come to on their own, in the evenings, on Saturdays and during the holidays. These will normally be for smaller audiences and the fees will be more moderate, but the speaker may be invited to give the same talk at several libraries.

There is need of advanced planning several months before, as the best speakers are heavily booked. There are several agencies for speakers but these tend to cater more for adult audiences. When arranging a programme for the first time, it is a good idea to talk to other children's librarians with this type of experience. Some museums and art galleries have excellent lecturers on their staff with considerable experience of talking to children. In education Her Majesty's inspectors and specialist advisers can give invaluable help and information on possible speakers. The British Association for the Advancement of Science, the Commonwealth Institute and different embassies have their own lists of speakers. For the library with a small budget these are extremely useful as they are subsidized by the organization concerned. Publishers usually have a good idea of authors and illustrators on their lists whom they feel would enjoy talking to a group of children.

It will have to be decided whether to arrange all the activities in a given period, as in a children's book festival or a national week, or whether to spread them throughout the year. The impact of an intensive week or fortnight can be more effective than events staged over a winter season. All schools will be invited to attend, exhibitions will be set up and a publicity campaign can be energetically carried out.

An imaginative and well-produced programme is needed, giving information on the speaker, the title, the subject of each session, and the time and the place when it is to be held. Information should also be given on the age group it is intended for, whether admission is by ticket and who to get them from, and whether a school class can come. Attractive publicity can arouse considerable interest and enthusiasm. Lambeth and Southwark have produced consistently good publicity in recent years. Further publicity can be obtained through the local and national press and local radio.

Musicians like Joseph Cooper and Sidney Harrison can be invited to play and discuss their music. Charles Gregory has introduced children to beautiful old guitars comparing them with the modern electric guitar, and James Blades and Joan Goossens have taken children on a *Journey through the Percussion Instruments of the Orchestra*.

Children in the Camden Junior Arts Festival have been escorted on a variety of visits to museums, theatres, art galleries and historic houses, and have attended comprehensive programmes in the libraries featuring the arts and sciences. Camden has a highly developed Library and Arts Department under the same director and the festival has developed from those run for children by the borough of St Pancras. Southwark has held several festivals of the arts for primary and secondary schools run by the youth librarian. Lambeth has an annual Children's Book Festival in their children's libraries in May each year. The programme is imaginative with strong emphasis on meeting authors, and new speakers are often featured.

Films used to be a popular feature in the winter evenings but in towns where there is a cinema it is difficult to obtain the films of the Children's Film Foundation. It is doubtful whether most of the films used were really worth showing; they attracted large audiences from a considerable distance but this was often the only time the children appeared in the library. It is better to have an occasional film of a book, providing it is well portrayed, or a film which is outstanding from a technical or historical point of view. It is hoped that the new venture, 'The Child's Own Theatre', which at present is starting under its Canadian name and which covers films, not live performances, will provide a worthwhile service. It is planned to have committees in each area and see previews of the proposed films. Film libraries are being built up, especially where the authority is also responsible for service to schools, and, apart from loaning films, libraries will show some to children, particularly in the sciences, and lecturers use films as part of their talks for children in the library. Metropolitan Toronto has a co-operative scheme in this field and exciting work is taking place in films and television at Cedarbrae, Scarboro.

Western Woods has some excellent motion pictures and filmstrips of picture books; these are useful with a large class of children or during the school holidays when there are too many children to group around the book conveniently. Copies of the book should be available so that the children can look at it again afterwards and take it home. Glass-beaded screens are particularly useful when filmstrips are being shown. When they are used the room does not have to be blacked out and can be used by other readers.

Regular talks are a feature in many libraries throughout the winter. Programmes are also held during the school holidays, in the evenings or on Saturday mornings, possibly alternating with a story hour. If space is limited tickets may be issued. The librarian will learn from experience approximately how many extra tickets to issue and which children will come. Subjects have to be chosen which appeal to children of many ages. Book illustrators have been extremely successful especially when they were prepared to draw for the children. Animals almost always guarantee success; probably some of the most interesting which have been in libraries were John Dixon's hawk and John Edwards's collection of snakes and reptiles, including an alligator. Children are fascinated to hear about film-making, especially if the lecturer illustrates his talk, as one did, with a film script, written and shot by children at a school. They can also be shown how to make things out of disposable objects found in every home; Pantopuck (E. R. Philpott) shows them how to make puppets and Avril Dankworth musical instruments. A short puppet show concludes Pantopuck's talk, and the children play Avril Dankworth's instruments. Constance Allen's dramatic presentation of characters from books is successful and her range is so wide that something can be selected for varying tastes and age groups.

Events may also be held throughout the school year for classes to attend. This has the advantage that the age group is stipulated and an audience is assured for events which children will enjoy but might be a little reluctant to attend on their own. When a company such as The Around Readers is being booked for a poetry reading, it would be disappointing and a waste of money if there was only a small audience and it would be difficult for the actors to receive sufficient group participation in the poetry. Barry Smith's programme *A Theatre of Puppets* using beautiful old and oriental puppets would not be appreciated by a crowd of young children who arrived expecting a puppet show. The problem with holding events in school hours is that children interested in a particular subject may not have the opportunity to come.

Some years ago children from several libraries in and around London were recorded at the BBC talking to authors about their books. These were broadcast in different parts of America to coincide with the publication of the American editions. During a National Library Week in Westminster, Philippa Pearce and Alan Garner were invited to the library to discuss their books with children. Manuscripts and illustrations were borrowed from the authors and publishers concerned. At each session two classes were invited and each class chose two spokesmen, a boy and a girl, who sat at the table with the author. Initially each school was asked to discuss one of the author's books so as to ensure that different questions were asked, but the discussions were open to the floor later in the proceedings. The children asked extremely perceptive questions and were fascinated to know how the authors had decided on the plot and whether the books were set in places where they had lived. Philippa Pearce's *Minnow on the Say* was extremely popular and they said that the boys were so real that she must have known them in life. It is necessary to warn authors that children may ask extremely frank questions, such as 'Were you the girl in that story?' and 'How did you feel when you were writing it?' Philippa Pearce, then Children's Book Editor of André Deutsch, was also asked many questions about the acceptance of manuscripts and whether they were all read when sent to publishers. The illustrations in some books were criticized, so in future sessions the illustrator and publisher were present whenever possible. Leon Garfield, Anthony Maitland and Patrick Hardy, Children's Book Editor of Longmans Young Books, have been particularly erudite and entertaining in discussing the work of making a book.

Puppetry has had a certain tradition in libraries and children's puppet groups have been formed or shows put on by members of staff. To embark on this type of project the staff must be somewhat talented. In areas where there are professionals readily available it is usually better to obtain their services for any shows required. There is little point in forming children's groups if they have one at school. The organizer needs experience and patience. A group was formed one summer for children who were continuously at the Queens Park Library, Westminster, and this was run by a professional puppeteer, Violet Philpott. The children made the puppets and the scenery, wrote the play and finally produced *Aladdin*.

Children's drama groups are popular in many libraries; the central library at Kensington has a nativity play annually, which is beautifully performed. In 1969 in the same programme Chelsea Library produced an excellent mummers' play.

Chess and stamp clubs may also be held, but they depend on

the knowledge of the person running them and tend to flop if there is a change of staff. There are the traditional entertainments for Hallowe'en like ghost stories told around a carved pumpkin, and possibly apple-bobbing.

Book clubs to encourage good reading are a feature in many children's libraries. A list of approved books is drawn up and a chart is put on the wall with the skeleton of a tree or a castle or some other symbol of attainment. As the child reads and discusses with the librarian the required number of books, his name is written on a brick or leaf and this is put on the chart; he probably progresses from red to silver and ultimately to gold. Then he is awarded a special badge or bookworms' certificate, which is sometimes sent to the school to be presented by the head teacher. This undoubtedly promotes good reading but the librarian must know the children and their capabilities extremely well, to avoid discouraging a slow reader, and it is difficult to be flexible and also fair.

Competitions are an inherent part of the programme of many book weeks and of National Library Week. The usual ones consist of writing a short story, a poem, dressing up as a character from a book, designing a book jacket or drawing a picture to illustrate a book. More unusual ones have been to do with local history, or making a peepshow portraying a scene from a book. Children made a Guy when Camden's Children's Arts Festival took place over the fifth of November. Children's arts and crafts competitions and exhibitions are also held. Some competitions are planned to involve the school, and class or group entries are submitted. It is necessary to examine motives closely. Does the library really want to foster a competitive spirit between schools? Prizes have to be spread around which means one cannot necessarily select the entries entirely on merit. All the submitted work should be shown in the local library so that all the children concerned can bring their parents and friends to view it.

FURTHER READING

Jolliffe, Harold. *Public Library Extension Activities*. 2nd edition. London, Library Association, 1962.

Chapter 10
The Library and the Special Needs of Different Groups in the Community

The library and a wide range of people working in the community have to co-operate to ensure that books become a normal part of life to children in their care.

Children under school age are dependent largely on their parents' interest as to whether or not books are available in their homes. A co-operative health visitor is in a position to persuade mothers to read books with their children. A health visitor may initiate a request for a list of books which would be suitable to read aloud. Children are often slow in talking, if there is a lack of communication between the child and the mother. Mothers' clubs are held weekly in many clinics and these are an excellent opportunity for the librarian to give a talk on books for the family, and on the services offered by all the departments. Of particular interest to mothers with young children will be story hours for under fives or a crèche to enable young children to be looked after at any time while the mother selects her own books.

Today it is possible to introduce books to many young children through playgroups, nursery schools and classes, and day nurseries. If the playgroup is sufficiently close to the library it is a good idea for the children to come for a story and to choose books for their playgroups. Children feel involved if they each choose a book which the leader may allow them to take home, especially if they have not yet got their own library tickets. The leader will also need help in selecting books which are suitable for story time, for action rhymes and games and perhaps some records of nursery rhymes. Books with simple ideas on how to make things are popular. Two members of staff on duty are desirable at the time of a playgroup visit so that both children and the leader can get adequate help in finding books. It is easier to issue all books to the playgroups than to individual children. Children who have their own tickets can then come

with their parents at other times. If the playgroup is too far
away or there are dangerous roads to cross it will be better to
take the books to the children. Books may be chosen by the
playgroup leader or the library may dispatch a box of perhaps
twenty specially selected books which can be changed at perhaps six weekly, or a maximum of a term's, intervals. The
library should keep a record of all books sent, each collection
should include a variety of stories and illustrations; nursery
rhymes and different titles should appear in subsequent collections. Whether or not the supervisor chooses her own books a
list should always be sent, and if it is left to the library to select
and send the books the playgroup should be advised when the
new books are to be delivered so that they have the old ones
ready for collection. When a large number of groups are served
by a centralized service it is easier to put the books initially
into collections and have lists of all collections duplicated so that
they are ready to go to the playgroups. On return they are
checked for withdrawals and the withdrawn book is replaced by
one of the same title. To operate this it is necessary to have
copies in reserve and each collection must include different
titles. Day nurseries in particular also use this as an approval
system for books which they may purchase themselves. Books
requested which are in the library stock will be added to the
next collection and also those which are required by staff, such
as books on child psychology and books on mentally and
physically handicapped children. It is necessary to ask that
children should be allowed to use the books themselves since
sometimes they are only used for story time and kept in their
box for the rest of the day. Clear pictures by good illustrators
from withdrawn books are useful for putting up on the walls of
new playgroups until they make some of their own. The older
children from day nurseries who are experienced in listening to
stories enjoy seeing a few of the Western Wood filmstrips
occasionally.

Children's librarians co-operate in courses for nursery nurses
and also those for playgroup leaders by talking about books for
the under fives, preferably in a children's library. Playgroup
staff are particularly grateful to be shown how to tell a story
to a group of children from a picture book. Book lists for children and publicity on the library service are useful as handouts.

Children in residential homes are usually encouraged to join their local library, but the home may also be glad of a loan collection to supplement their own stock of books. The children usually go to local schools, but very emotionally disturbed children may be taught in the home and come as a group for regular library visits. They tend to cover a fairly wide age and ability range, and some children are backward because of either lack of schooling through illness or conditions in their own homes. Books such as 'The Inner Ring' or 'Jet' Series are helpful for older children with reading difficulties as the subjects chosen are not childish. It is essential for the librarian to get to know each one in the group as an individual so that she can recommend books which have relevance. All types of sport, books on animals, carpentry for boys, clothes for girls are popular; in fact interests cover the normal range of children though the concentration span is often very limited. Whether or not to give a book talk or tell a story will depend on the age and ability of the children in the group and whether there are sufficient staff available to help. A record of the siege of Troy was used in Canada with a group of disturbed children of between nine and thirteen. Excited by the story, the children expressed amazement that it came from a book. It is helpful if the adult library is adjacent or if both children's and adults' books are in the same room, as older children particularly will prefer to borrow books from that section.

Little provision appears to be made in some areas for children in hospital, neither the Red Cross nor the public library provides a service. Kent County Library and Lewisham run a service to children in hospital and there are qualified hospital librarians in some hospitals such as the National Hospital. As the hospital librarian is a member of a team of therapists concerned with the well-being and care of the patient it is better if she, rather than a children's librarian from the local library, attends to the child in hospital. When she has little experience in children's literature she will be grateful for advice on the purchase of children's books for the hospital library, and possibly for an exchange collection to boost her own stock and advice on books to suit the needs of particular patients. The library should also have books for all ages to prepare children for admission to hospital, but care should be taken that the subject is portrayed in an interesting way, though not glamorized, and that the children are prepared for unpleasant routines such as blood tests, X-rays and injections, and for pleasant things such as visitors and presents.

New hospitals are now being built with children's units rather than separate buildings, so the hospital library for patients who are able to move around should also have furniture suitable for children, low shelves and kinderboxes as in the public library. If the floor is carpeted the children will be able to sit on it. As in the libraries of schools for the physically handicapped there should be adequate space for children in wheel-chairs to reach the shelves and tables of correct height so that books may be placed there and the wheel-chair drawn up to the table.

Patients in bed may need aids to enable them to read, like book rests, which can be fitted to a bedside table, prismatic or mirror spectacles, and microfilm readers which may be operated by a hand switch. The librarian will seek advice from the hospital staff on which reading aid will be most suitable for the patient. The trolley service may visit the ward once or twice weekly and there should be a cupboard on each ward holding a variety of books for children, so that they will not be without books until the trolley comes again.

The child entering hospital who is not critically ill may be comforted to see some familiar books and to meet new ones. R. A. Mitchell, a teacher at Queen Mary's Hospital, Carshalton, discussed the problem of the long-stay children who tend to forget there is a world outside the hospital: 'For our youngest children this real world which contains so few real objects and experiences is very limiting. This is why our two year olds have a full-time nursery teacher. This is why they must have films and books even at so young an age, this is why they must be put into prams and taken out to see things like motor cars and tractors and pigs and trees.'[1] Thus in hospital a young child needs books so that he can experience the everyday life of a child with his family and his own possessions. *Wake Up Farm* by Alvin Tresselt, and *Papa Small* by Lois Lenski, are particularly useful. The child in hospital and the physically handicapped child want to be like everybody else, and experience, even indirectly, through books or films, those things that they are unable to accomplish. Many perfectly healthy children also have a similar wish fulfilment in wanting books about football players or 'pop' stars.

When a child is physically inactive the librarian can introduce books which will satisfy a quest for knowledge and stimulate interest in reading. Handicapped children are at a disadvantage when they meet and compete with normal people later in life and it is vital that the child is given the opportunity to develop his intellectual powers to the best of his ability. Close co-operation to this end is essential between the hospital librarian and his teacher. Children who are physically handicapped may have multiple handicaps and those who have been ill for long periods may be backward. On the other hand they may be extremely intelligent. There is a poignant article by Prudence Sutherland on a severely handicapped girl; it is about her loneliness, her fears and her search for her own identity through literature as an adolescent.[2]

Play leaders will need books for story time and books which will give ideas for action games. Occupational therapists and psychologists will also need help from the librarian in finding books to help their patients come to terms with their problems. In a paper on bibliotherapy, Mrs J. Andrewes said that reading a story aloud forced the child to concentrate on something other than himself.[3]

The National Library for the Blind caters for non-sighted children by supplying books in braille free of charge. Local authorities assist by contributing an annual fee for persons resident in their area. New titles for children are brailled each year, they are expensive to produce and are much larger than their printed counterparts, *The Grange at High Force* by Philip Turner is in four volumes, but they also last considerably longer. The children attend special schools. An interesting experiment is to include in a few braille books the printed text and illustrations. These books would appear to have particular value in a family where there are sighted and non-sighted children. *The Braille Library Bulletin* is published six times a year in ink print and braille and gives a synopsis of new books. The National Library for the Blind also includes books in large print for partially-sighted readers. Unlike books in braille these are not post-free and they are supplied through public libraries. The Ulverscroft series and the Rylee series are available in most public libraries but these are supplemented by the Keith Jennison series which is available from the National Library for the Blind. The books are very attractively produced and children's titles include *Aesop's Fables, Arabian Nights, National Velvet, Alice's Adventures in Wonderland, A Tale of Two Cities, Some Merry Adventures of Robin Hood, Tom Sawyer* and *The Odyssey.*

Talking books are supplied by the Royal National Institute for the Blind but are not available to persons under twenty-one years of age. They are used with children in the United States and in Sweden. In Sweden they are felt to be the future book for the blind. They are now recorded on tape rather than on records and the recipient will require a tape-recorder at home or in hospital. Talking books would also be of value to other children in hospital as an alternative to microfilm.

Miss M. I. Ashworth, a speech therapist, discussed the problems of the deaf at the 1969 Youth Libraries Group weekend school.[4] Some children are born deaf and never hear spoken words; others have defective hearing so their conception of speech is blurred. Their vocabulary is thus limited and they may also be retarded. Picture books can be used as a source of vocabulary but drawings should be explicit and clear and the entire story must be portrayed through the illustration as in any good picture book.

At the same weekend school Mr L. Bartup discussed the need of similar illustration for autistic children and stressed that they must comprehend what they are reading.[5] These children do not appear to wish to communicate and symptoms include the absence or delay of speech development. The cause is not fully known.

Mentally handicapped children can gain considerable benefit from books and the library. The handicap varies from educationally sub-normal children to severely handicapped children. In Westminster there are two day nurseries for young mentally handicapped children and a special school with a close relationship with these and the library. Mentally handicapped children can enjoy the same picture books and stories as other children and can participate in library affairs including story time with normal children. Older educationally sub-normal children respond in an extremely rewarding manner to books which they could not undertake themselves, but which are read aloud to them in the library. These children should be included in special activities. Particularly successful are events with a strong audio or visual approach like *The Asian Music Circle*, a demonstration of dances from the Indian sub-continent, or James Blades' and Joan Goossens' *Journey through the Percussion Instruments of the Orchestra*.

Libraries must cater for the backward reader, but it is difficult to find the best way of doing so. Some libraries have a special collection in the adult lending library intended for teenagers and adults, and another collection in the children's library. Needless to say these should not be labelled as for backward readers. Sometimes a star is put on the books and only the children with a similar star on their tickets may borrow them, but unfortunately other children will soon realize why there is a star on these tickets.

A wide range of reading schemes for backward readers is available as shown in *The Reluctant Reader*, 1969,[6] and the National Book League's *Help in Reading*, 1968.[7] The library may already stock the 'Ladybird Easy Reading Books' and the 'Jet Books', the 'Inner Ring' and the ITA 'A Chance To Read' series for older age groups, and other schemes, but well-meaning parents may do more harm than good by trying to help a child to read something he is not ready for which they have selected at the library. Advice should be sought from the child's teacher and the remedial teacher, and children are often encouraged to take their reading book home from school.

The essence of this service is for the librarian to build up a personal relationship with the children concerned. She should arrange to visit the school at the time the remedial group is meeting to encourage the children to join the library, and if possible to visit the library regularly as a group. By story-telling and reading aloud she can present material which the children will enjoy but could not tackle themselves.

The co-operation of parents should also be encouraged, possibly by inviting them and the teachers to an open evening at the library so that they may be aware that the library staff wish to help their children. A display of books may be set up and a relevant book list distributed.

Libraries where there is good staffing, and where children are known, may prefer to keep all books in the normal sequence

5

except for any definite reading scheme which may be on restricted access. They may rely on building up a friendship between the child and the librarian. It also helps to give the child confidence if he is encouraged to become a library helper.

The librarian needs to know her stock and duplicate in sufficient quantity those books which are also suitable for backward readers, especially in fiction. When reading and reviewing books this problem should be especially considered. Unfortunately many of the very simple stories have texts which would be suitable if it was not for pictures of a very young child or some remark implying the age of a young child in the text. The sheer nonsense of *The Cat in the Hat* and some of the 'Beginner Books' are enjoyed and the early 'I Can Read Books' are also popular. Suitable books can also be found amongst the Hamish Hamilton 'Antelope Series', such as *Truce of the Games* by Rosemary Sutcliff, and *Dragon Come Home* by Janet McNeil. Some of the 'Acorns', like *The Castle of Yew* by Lucy M. Boston, are also suitable for children who can read but are below their normal reading age.

The 'Jackanory Series' have large clear print. *Robin Hood*, adapted by Edward Blishen is extremely successful as are others, especially if the children have seen the programme on television. Fairy-stories are enjoyed; the re-tellings of Virginia Haviland are attractive to all children, and the printing and format are inviting. Other single fairy-stories such as *Mr Miacca*, illustrated by Evaline Ness, are valuable. Parents should be encouraged to read aloud standard books like *The Lion, the Witch and the Wardrobe* by C. S. Lewis so that the child does not miss them. Special tickets should be issued to parents so that both the child and parents have the opportunity to choose a suitable selection.

It is frequently easier to arouse the child's interest in non-fiction than fiction. Suitable material is presented in an uncomplicated way, the printing is well spaced and there are explanatory illustrations. The 'Let's Read and Find Out About Science' series of A. C. Black, the 'Ladybird Easy Reading' series, 'People at Work', 'Stand and Stare', a nature series published by Methuen, and the 'Junior True Books' published by Muller all include titles which have been particularly successful with backward readers.

The Bodley Head's beautifully illustrated series 'Natural Science Picture Books' are enjoyed especially, as these children are often particularly interested in animals. *Shackleton's Epic Voyage,* and *First Up Everest,* illustrated by Raymond Briggs, are invaluable. The children should be shown beautiful illustrated books even if they cannot read them like *Shakespeare's Theatre* by Walter Hodges.

The Initial Teaching Alphabet Books should be shelved in a separate section in the library and labelled ITA. This method of teaching is sometimes used with the remedial reading groups in junior schools when children have failed to learn to read in infants' school. ITA books will also be required for little children learning to read by this method, and the library should stock ITA versions of books, which are in the normal stock. The quantity will depend on the number of children using ITA but all libraries should have a few, even if local schools do not use it, for children moving into the district who may have been learning to read by this method.

When dealing with backward readers it is most important to get to know the children and their interests, and to show the individual child books he will enjoy. Paperbacks have an important place with backward and reluctant readers, as they look easier, and will often be borrowed while the hardback remains on the shelves. Records may also help to keep an interest in the library, especially if the child enjoys music.

In 1969 at the Annual General Meeting of the Youth Libraries Group[8] and at the Weekend School,[9] speakers discussed the gifted child, how to recognize such a child, and how librarians could help to meet the child's needs. The child's reading age may be much higher than his chronological or emotional age. Outstanding talent takes several forms; it may be academic, creative, technical or social. These children are a problem for their parents and continually ask difficult questions. From a very young age they badly need books on an extremely wide range of topics. Macdonald publish several graded series which are extremely useful to parents, particularly with reference to the scientific type of question. As librarians we should see that the advanced child does not miss the opportunity of reading the outstanding books in children's literature. A problem sometimes arises when the gifted child borrows adult novels for which he is emotionally insufficiently mature. A sympathetic librarian can fulfil a need to communicate by discussing books and a child's interests with him. Gifted children should not be restricted in the number of books borrowed within reason, and should be allowed to use all the library departments if they wish. Activities in the library in which they could work with other children are also useful. The Association for Gifted Children runs its own special clubs, but local branches should be kept informed of all library activities and offered any other co-operation required.

Foreign children resident in England and immigrant children require special consideration in stock provision. Young children tend to learn English quickly from other children at school and are frequently reading at a normal level in their class in a surprisingly short time. Parents of children not yet at school who have no playmates of a similar age are sometimes worried about the child's lack of English, and will come into the library to ask for books to help him. Here it is of benefit to suggest taking the child to a playgroup so that he will meet and talk with other children before going to school. Picture books with illustrations of objects giving the name beside them are useful as are alphabet books, as long as the whole word is written out and not just the initial. Nursery rhymes are very much part of our heritage and it will help if the child knows some of them. The child will also be able to follow stories through pictures, if his picture books are selected with care. Story time at the library, *Listen With Mother* on the radio and *Play School* on television will help the child develop his vocabulary, and at the library he will meet other children.

Teenagers have more problems in learning the language than younger children and when reading English at first will require the type of books previously mentioned with an older interest range. Some suitable titles will also be found in the 'Topliners' and 'Pyramid' series. There may also be a special case here for some of the abridged editions of classics published by Longmans. I do feel that these should only be available for those with a reading or language problem and are probably better housed in the adult section.

Books are also needed in the vernacular, particularly for this age group so that they have the opportunity to read books relevant to their own life and culture. For the older children it is possible to obtain books in European languages from other libraries in the Language Specialisation Scheme. This should be extended to cover books suitable for all ages. Birmingham is setting up an Indian and Pakistani language library and circulating collections of adult books in specified languages, which are to be made available in other libraries on a subscription basis. Young children should be encouraged to keep their heritage and books should be made available in the vernacular wherever there is a sufficiently large linguistic group, particularly when the community is attempting to preserve its own culture and to have its children taught their own language after school. There are a few specialized bookshops like Zeno in Soho for Greek books. Help in selection may be obtained from foreign cultural attachés, foreign librarians, international organizations like the International Youth Library and large libraries in the countries concerned. New York Public Library makes special provision for the city's large Spanish-speaking population and can be of help for the Spanish language.

All books should be selected carefully and should not be included when they are inaccurate, or prejudicial towards any race, nationality or religion. A working party of the London and Home Counties Branch has made a critical examination of books on selected countries.[10] Older classics reflect the attitude of their time, and although these have a place in literature the same ideas are not always acceptable in books of today. In a study carried out in several countries of children's views of foreign peoples by Wallace E. Lambert and Otto Klineberg it was shown that adults often taught children prejudice through their own ignorance; television had a great influence in the way it depicted other countries and their peoples, and so to a lesser, but vital extent, did books.[11] More books with immigrant characters are needed, of the calibre of Ezra Keats's picture books in which the everyday life of an ordinary American Negro family is portrayed and collections of folktales like *Tales of an Ashanti Father* collected by Peggy Appiah. Judith Elkin discussed at the short course at Leeds her work with immigrants at Birmingham, and how she had selected books from the normal library stock for teachers to use with children who were learning English as a second language. Two teachers from different areas assessed their success with each book, and an exhibition was set up at a teaching centre of the books with the teachers' comments. The book list has been published.[12]

Children should also be given the opportunity to see some of the traditional culture of other lands. The Westminster Council of Social Service has twice organized a People to People week. Most of the events consisted of visits to places of interest for students and adults and 'at homes' were held at different organizations and in private homes. The Westminster Overseas Committee was extremely helpful in suggesting people to come to the children's libraries and one event with two Indian dancers in exotic costumes dancing beautifully completely captivated both boys and girls. The Commonwealth Institute is also very helpful in arranging speakers from other countries. The women immigrants are often lonely and it is sometimes possible to reach them through their children. Contact with community representatives is vital and if people are shy to come to us we must go to them. Small collections of books could be lent to people in their own homes and could be freely circulated by them to their neighbours and friends.

There was considerable concern over provision for adolescents in the early days of public libraries; the children's reading rooms catered mainly for them. There have been endless arguments about whether they are best catered for as a section of the adult library or in the children's library, in an intermediate library or with no separate special provision at all. There is frequently too little co-ordination in book selection to enable books to be found in both departments which act as a bridge to mature reading. Some authors appearing on children's publishing lists, like Leon Garfield, Alan Garner, Katherine Peyton, V. Brinsmead, and Hester Burton, will be enjoyed equally by adults. J. D. Salinger's *The Catcher in the Rye* and William Golding's *Lord of the Flies* have a place in the older readers' section of the children's library.

In the United States there appears to be some movement away from the separate teenage library and the danger of creating a vacuum is discussed by Kenneth R. Shaffer.[13] Attempts have been made to provide especially for teenagers at Lincoln, Walsall and West Norwood, Lambeth. At Lincoln the aim is to attract the non-reading teenagers into the library. Pop music is played all the time it is open and records may be borrowed. An experiment was carried out with hardbacks and paperbacks and it was found that 75 per cent of the stock issued was in paperback. Lincoln has also concentrated on providing displays; there are psychedelic soft furnishings and cushions, and the staff are young.[14] Walsall does not staff the teenage library which is placed between the adult and the children's library with glass screening. Young people go to the children's library for help. They concentrate on fiction which young people enjoy and non-fiction geared to the syllabuses of the CSE and GCE examinations and in the type of non-fiction which interest teenagers particularly like sociology, hobbies, and sports. But the young people are encouraged to use the entire library. Private study rooms are provided and also general areas in the main room. It is sometimes suggested that it is with the study area that the most useful provision can be made for this age group. At Walsall there is a library club whose members make comments on the books on approval and do reviews for their magazines. An annotated book list is published including adult and children's titles in consultation with local teachers and school librarians.[15] West Norwood teenage library is not separately staffed. The area is informal, there are excellent facilities for display and music is sometimes played. A committee of young staff members and readers choose books to place there but there is no permanent stock. Tasteful informality should entice readers to all parts of this building, and it has the potential to be a dynamic cultural centre in the community.

Librarians cannot afford to be complacent and there are no good excuses for so many young people ceasing to use the library. Where libraries are modern in design, and the staff in them are alert and enthusiastic, they are better used by teenagers. In the first place we must make reading a worthwhile personal experience in the child's life in the school and in the junior library, through building up of good stock, well-balanced and in sufficient quantity for a reasonable choice to be always available. Then staff must be on hand who can make books live, formally through book talks but also by discussing them with the individual child in the library. Children should be taught how to use books in their studies and in pursuit of their own interests. Where there are separate departments, buildings should be planned so that staff are not tied to the mechanics of book charging and can readily go between departments with readers. At busy periods after school when young people tend to come into the library, every available member of staff should be put on duty in the public departments and rather than have large queues developing around the enquiry desk, staff should walk about to see if anyone is in need of help. Often people will approach the librarian and say that they did not like to trouble the person at the desk. Small duplicated plans of the layout of the stock are helpful and special care should be taken with the guiding. Annotated book lists are useful as an addition to, but not as a substitute for, readers' advisers. Reviews of books by young people like *Opinion* in Toronto are another useful means of promotion. Imaginative grouping of books in enterprising displays can also 'sell' books which might be lost on the shelves and older children can set up some unusual and interesting displays. Some young people would welcome an opportunity to be similarly involved in the adult library. In Sweden and the United States exciting programmes are arranged in the evenings or during school holidays, including talks by authors and lectures on music, theatre, films, fashion, sports and technology. Lively book clubs have been held, young people have discussed books and current affairs on radio and television. In Finland at Tampere Public Library there is a Youth Theatre which aims to interest young people in the theatre; several of the actors have later made it their career.[16] Activities for adolescents must be of current interest; there was a stimulating summer programme at Skokil, Illinois,[17] for the twelve to fourteen age group entitled *Quest*. One session was called 'Conformity versus Non-Conformity' and used a multi-media approach including psychedelic music which endeavoured to bring books to life. In Harlem young people presented their own poetry to other young adults.[18]

In America there have been problems over the high school students in the library, and the crowding out of adult readers. Although there is now increased student use there have been fewer difficulties where library authorities have provided larger budgets and expanded book-selection policies to meet student needs, have increased staff and space, and where school libraries have been further developed and opening hours increased. The Knapp School Libraries Project, by building up a very few selected schools to meet the National Standards for school libraries, and by working with the teaching faculties in the university concerned and demonstrating the educational value of a well-developed school library to visitors from many school boards, and to teachers and librarians, resulted in an awareness and improvement in the libraries in many other schools throughout the United States.[19]

In Britain, developing comprehensive education will result in resource centres full of books and other types of audio-visual materials. Better facilities in the schools will result in more informed use of the public library service but the public library must be ready and able to meet the demand. Staffing facilities are important and the educational needs of young people should be further considered in stock acquisition by all departments. Vertical files of current information should be maintained and quick photo-copying should be available immediately on demand, so that the two services will complement each other. Computer catalogues giving readily available subject lists and a location list at every service-point are invaluable when a book is wanted immediately. Telex is a speedy way of getting information from another library. The teenagers' needs for information are usually immediate. As we mechanize our routine processes and install speedier methods of communication, more staff can be spared from behind the scenes to provide a more efficient service to readers.

The teenager has many calls on his free time and the library must go out into the community to reach those who do not come to us. Youth clubs are sometimes glad of help in the form of suggestions as to which books to buy with their own allowances and in supplementary loan collections from the library. These will include a wide range of fiction and popular non-fiction for reading at home, but also books which give assistance to work being done in the club or youth centre such as boat building, dress designing, sports, cookery, and of course play sets and books on drama. Activities can be carried on at youth centres, with the library arranging for a speaker and setting up book exhibitions. Audrey Slaughter, the editor of *Honey*, gave a talk to a group of girls at a Paddington Youth Centre who were designing and making clothes. She said that to be interesting, young women must cultivate a wide range of interests and that reading would help them. Later in the year the library staff were invited to a very professional mannequin parade of the garments the girls had made. Libraries can also hold coffee evenings to introduce the library to young people from youth clubs. In some places where the children's libraries are in a separate building or room older children in the junior library are given an invitation to visit the main library at a prearranged time singly or in a small group so that a member of the adult staff will be available to show them around and get to know them.

An activity or club room with pegboard fittings on the walls to hold books, interspersed with large hessian display areas would be invaluable in many areas. It could be used by different sections of the community at different times with relevant books and displays being set up as required. Facilities could be built in for record and tape-playing, showing of films, and serving refreshments. If the room can be divided by movable screens to accommodate small or large audiences, or serve as a meeting room or to hold an exhibition, the use will be extremely flexible. Young people could meet their friends there, have discussions on varying topics, hold classical music and pop sessions, and watch films in an informal setting. A selection of books and other material may be useful in introducing them to the services available in the library.

In America attempts have been made to reach the non-reader by going out to places where young people congregate; to the beach or swimming pool, for example, with paperbacks and records. In East Baltimore a Volkswagen bus was used and paperbacks were displayed inside and outside, films were shown and records played.[20] Students of the University of Maryland School of Library and Information Services set up an informal library in a converted house in a deprived area.[21] An extremely interesting experiment took place at a summer camp for disturbed children, children from slum areas and juvenile delinquents at the University of Michigan Fresh Air Camp. It was an attempt to see whether children – mainly with a non-reading background – would read where there were many other activities including swimming, boating, hiking, fishing and a craftshop. On the first day each child was taken to the library and asked to choose two paperbacks as a present which he could change for others in the library or with other campers. The amount of time the campers were seen reading was recorded. The teenagers read most even though more of their time was taken by helping younger children in other activities and, although they had had little interest when they arrived, reading became popular.[22]

There is co-operation between librarians and probation officers; collections of books are lent so that the probation officer can give them to young people in his care. Paperbacks, particularly of fiction would be useful here, as often the non-fiction is better used. Many young people prefer a paperback and the books are cheaper and more easily expendable.

An interest in reading which is retained in adult life will be helped by the imaginative book selection and stock maintenance of both public and school library services and by the way in which books are used and introduced to children by teachers and librarians. Daniel Fader's *Hooked on Books* is an invaluable illustration of how books can be studied in depth with less able children and made relevant to their own lives.[23]

REFERENCES

1 R. A. Mitchell. 'The Hospital and the Child' in *Reading and Health. Papers given at the Hospital Libraries and Handicapped Readers Group Conference and Week-End School . . . 1965*. London, the Hospital Libraries and Handicapped Readers Group, 1967. pp. 21–9.

2 Prudence A. Sutherland. 'On the Need of the Severely Handicapped To Feel that They Are Human'. *Top of the News*, vol. 25, no. 3, April 1969. pp. 263–7.

3 Mrs J. Andrewes. 'Bibliotherapy' in *Reading and Health* . . . pp. 42–51 (see note 1 above).

4 M. I. Ashworth. 'Youth Libraries Group Week-end School, 1969.' *Youth Libraries Group News*, vol. 13, no. 2, October 1969.

5 L. Bartup. Ibid.

6 Library Association. County Libraries Group. *The Reluctant Reader*. Reader's guide. New series, no. 111. 3rd edition. London, Library Association, 1969.

7 National Book League. *Help in Reading: Books for the Teacher of Backward Children and for Pupils Backward in Reading* . . . by J. C. Daniels . . . and S. S. Segal. 4th edition. London, National Book League, 1968.

8 Mrs V. H. Mitten. 'The Gifted Child'. *Youth Libraries Group News*, vol. 13, no. 2, June 1969.

9 R. R. Stewart. 'Youth Libraries Group Week-End School, 1969'. *Youth Libraries Group News*, vol. 13, no. 2, October 1969.

10 Janet Hill (ed.). *Books for Children: the Homelands of Immigrants to Britain.* London, Institute of Race Relations (Special Series), 1971.

11 Wallace E. Lambert and Otto Klineberg. *Children's Views of Foreign Peoples: A Cross National Study.* New York, Appleton Century Crofts, 1967. Review by Leigh Minturn in *Wilson Library Bulletin*, October 1967. pp. 187–93.

12 Judith Elkin. *Books for the Multi-Racial Classroom.* Library Association Pamphlet no. 10. London, Library Association, Youth Libraries Group, 1972.

13 Kenneth R. Shaffer. 'What Makes Sammy Read'. *Top of the News*, vol. 19, March 1963. pp. 9–12.

14 Christine Knight. 'Lincoln City Teenage Library'. *Youth Libraries Group News*, vol. 13, no. 2, June 1969.

15 Maureen White. 'Walsall Teenage Library'. *Youth Libraries Group News*, vol. 13, no. 2, June 1969.

16 Maija Liisa Peltonen. 'The Youth Theatre of the Library' in *Library Service to Young Adults*, edited by Emma Cohn and Brita Olsson. Published by the Public Libraries Section of IFLA. Copenhagen, Bibliotekscentralen, 1968. pp. 55–60.

17 Sandra Stroner and Florence Burmeister. 'Summer Happenings'. *Top of the News*, vol. 25, no. 3, April 1969. pp. 291–300.

18 Lydia Lafleur. 'Poetry Evenings in Harlem'. *Top of the News*, vol. 24, no. 1, November 1967. pp. 42–6.

19 *Impact: the School Library and the Instructional Program. A Report on Phase I of the Knapp School Libraries Project* by Peggy Sullivan. Chicago, American Library Association, 1967. *Realization: the Final Report of the Knapp School Libraries Project* edited by Peggy Sullivan. Chicago, American Library Association, c. 1968.

20 Pauline Winnick. 'Young People in Libraries'. *Catholic Library World*, vol. 39, October 1967. pp. 128–32.

21 High John. *Library Journal*, vol. 93, no. 2, 15 January 1968. pp. 147–55.

22 Elton B. McNeil. 'What I Done Last Summer' in *Hooked on Books* by Daniel Fader. Oxford, Pergamon Press, 1966.

23 'Study Guides for West Side Story' by Irvine Shulman and 'Anne Frank: The Diary of a Young Girl' in *Hooked on Books* by Daniel Fader. Oxford, Pergamon Press, 1966. pp. 92–126.

FURTHER READING

Bannister, Sheila. 'The Library and the Teenager'. *The Assistant Librarian Symposium*, vol. 56, no. 6, July 1963. pp. 106–28.

Barnes, Melvyn P. *Youth Library Work.* London, Clive Bingley, 1968.

Beswick, Norman W. 'The School Library and the Highly Gifted Child'. *School Librarian*, vol. 17, no. 4, December 1969. pp. 293–9.

Crouch, Marcus. 'Work with Disabled Children and Slow Learners' in *Hospital Libraries and Work with the Disabled* compiled by Mona Going. London, Library Association, 1963. pp. 155–61.

Frommer, E. D. *The Needs of Children in Hospital in Reading and Health . . .* London, The Hospital Libraries and Handicapped Readers Group, 1967.

Heffernan, Virginia (ed.), 'The Exceptional Child'. Several articles in *Top of the News*, vol. 25, no. 3, April 1969. pp. 261–90.

Lambert, Claire M. 'Library Provision for the Indian and Pakistani Communities in Britain'. *Journal of Librarianship*, vol. 1, no. 1, January 1969. pp. 41–61.

Lewis, M. Joy. 'The Hospital Librarian and the Child' in *International Federation of Library Associations Library Service to Children*, vol. 2. pp. 82–5 and bibliography.

Rollins, Charlemae. 'The Role of the Book in Combating Prejudice'. *Wilson Library Bulletin*, vol. 42, no. 2, October 1967. pp. 176–9.

RECOMMENDED BOOKS

Appiah, Peggy. *Tales of An Ashanti Father*. London, André Deutsch, 1967.

Blishen, Edward. *Robin Hood*. Jackanory. London, BBC, 1969.

Boston, Lucy M. *The Castle of Yew*. London, The Bodley Head, 1967.

Briggs, Raymond. *First Up Everest*. London, Hamish Hamilton, 1969.

Briggs, Raymond. *Shackleton's Epic Voyage*. London, Hamish Hamilton, 1969.

Golding, William. *Lord of the Flies*. London, Faber, 1954.

Hodges, Walter. *Shakespeare's Theatre*. London, Oxford University Press, 1964.

Lenski, Lois. *Papa Small*. London, Oxford University Press, 1957.

Lewis, C. S. *The Lion, the Witch and the Wardrobe*. London, Bles, 1950.

MacNeil, Janet. *Dragon Come Home*. Antelope. London, Hamish Hamilton, 1969.

Ness, Evaline. *Mr Miacca*. London, The Bodley Head, 1968.

Salinger, J. D. *The Catcher in the Rye*. London, Hamish Hamilton, 1951.

Seuss, Dr. *The Cat in the Hat*. London, Collins, 1961.

Sutcliff, Rosemary. *Truce of the Games*. Antelope. London, Hamish Hamilton, 1971.

Tresselt, Alvin. *Wake Up Farm*. Tadworth, World's Work, 1966.

Series

'A Chance To Read'. Girl's and boy's set. Initial Teaching Publishing Company.

'Acorn'. The Bodley Head.

'Antelope'. Hamish Hamilton.

'First Library'. Macdonald.

'Inner Ring'. Benn.

'Jackanory'. BBC.

'Jet Books'. Cape.

'Junior True Books'. Muller.
'Ladybird Easy Reading'. Wills and Hepworth.
'Let's Read and Find Out about Science'. A. & C. Black.
'Natural Science Picture Books'. The Bodley Head.
'New Method Supplementary'. Longman.
'Pyramid Books'. Heinemann Educational.
'Simplified English'. Longman.
'Stand and Stare'. Methuen.
'Starters'. Macdonald.
'Structural Readers'. Longman.
'Topliners'. Macmillan.

Large Print Books
Keith Jennison Series.
Rylee Series.
Ulverscroft Series.

Chapter 11
National and International Organizations Concerned with Children and Their Reading

National and international organizations are concerned with providing books for children, some of them historical but most concerned with problems facing us today.

In Britain there is a Children's Writers Group which is a part of the Society of Authors. Meetings are held on a variety of topics of interest to their members and others working with books like publishers and librarians are sometimes invited to attend.

The Children's Book Group is a group within the Publishers Association with its own executive committee. It is especially concerned with children's books and organizes the annual Children's Book Show. It also participates as a group at the Bologna Children's Book Fair each year and at the Biennale of Book Illustrations at Bratislava. Financial support comes from the group and from the Board of Trade.

The Children's Book Circle is an informal body of children's book editors who hold monthly meetings and discussions. Stimulating joint meetings are held from time to time with the London and Home Counties branch of the Youth Libraries Group. The Eleanor Farjeon Award is given annually by this group to a person who has given distinguished service in the field of children's books. Award winners have included Margery Fisher, Jessica Jenkins, formerly of the National Book League, Brian Alderson, Anne Wood of the Federation of Children's Book Groups, Kaye Webb, the editor of Puffin Books, who has made an enormous contribution to providing books of quality at prices a child can afford from his own pocket money, and Janet Hill, in recognition of her work in editing the assessed list of books about the homelands of immigrants.[1]

The Youth Libraries Group, founded as the Youth Libraries Section in 1947, is a part of the Library Association open to all members who work with, or are interested in, children and young people. They commented on the inadequate services for children in their surveys of 1954 and 1958–59 and appended to the latter a memorandum on the duties of children's librarians. There are local branches in different parts of the country which hold a variety of meetings, one-day schools and co-operative working party ventures on, for example, the investigation into the wear of children's books.[2]

Local group meetings are extremely helpful both professionally and socially especially to children's librarians who may be working very much in isolation. An annual weekend school is held in September and specialists working in different ways with children are invited to speak. It is open to anyone interested in children and reading, whether or not they are members, so authors and publishers also attend.

The Library Association awards two prizes annually; the Carnegie and the Kate Greenaway Medals. The Carnegie Award (1936) is open to any book which is published for the first time in the United Kingdom during the previous year. It is for a book of distinction which may be fiction or non-fiction. The Kate Greenaway Award (1955) is awarded for outstanding illustration of a children's book which was first published in the United Kingdom during the previous year. Artists like Edward Ardizzone, Brian Wildsmith, John Burningham, Raymond Briggs and Charles Keeping have been recognized, but also book illustrators for older children, for instance Pauline Baynes for *A Dictionary of Chivalry*.

The Youth Libraries Group now has its own publications programme which has included pamphlets on book reviewing,[3] book selection,[4] and recommended book lists.[5]

The School Library Association was founded in 1937 to promote the use of the school library and books in school as a means of education. The school library section of the Library Association also founded in 1937 amalgamated with the School Library Association in 1946. There are branches in different parts of the country and it includes institutional and personal members. It provides a professional interchange of experience through meetings and has published good book lists and an excellent periodical, the *School Librarian*, which is valued by all who work with books both for its articles and its excellent reviews. A weekend school is held annually and is attended by

teachers, teacher-librarians, librarians and publishers. It co-
operates locally with branches of the Youth Libraries Group
holding joint meetings, and in 1958 the School Library
Association and the Library Association organized a joint
certificate in librarianship to practising teachers.

The National Book League is an independent body registered
as an educational charity which raises funds by subscription
from personal and corporate members. Its headquarters are at
7 Albemarle Street, London, WI, where book exhibitions on
different themes are held. There is also a library and a permanent display of new books from the previous twelve months
which are donated by publishers. Many of its exhibitions and
book lists are geared to school needs and travelling exhibitions
from the National Book League may be borrowed by schools,
colleges and libraries. A catalogue is also available. The
Education and Exhibitions Department is responsible for this
work and investigates problems in the supply of books in particular fields and makes recommendations for book expenditure
in schools.

The need for a National Centre for children's literature was
discussed by Brian Alderson and John Townsend of the British
Museum at the Library Association conference in September
1968.[6] The speakers considered how existing services like the
British Museum, National Book League and Youth Libraries
Group could be increased. The North London Polytechnic
School of Librarianship is endeavouring to establish a research
appointment to consider the establishment of a centre. There is
a need for a comprehensive collection of children's books of all
periods to be readily available to the student and with staff to
exploit them. Bibliographies of the collection of old books in the
British Museum and other libraries are needed both nationally
and internationally. The catalogue[7] of the Osborne collection of
early children's books, 1566–1910, is an invaluable bibliographic tool which is supplemented by a list of additions in *A
Chronicle of Boys' and Girls' House*, 1969, and includes a list of
books in the Lillian H. Smith collection which starts from
1911.[8] Lance Salway has edited a guide, published by the Youth
Libraries Group on special collections in London and the Home
Counties.[9] The 'Friends of the Osborne and Lillian H. Smith
Collections' has been established in Britain to spread knowledge

of these collections and to enable people with a common interest in children's libraries to meet and work together.

The Library of Congress after a report in 1952 by Frances Clarke-Sayers on the children's books there, recognized the need for a children's book section,[10] and established one under the General Reference and Bibliography Division in March 1963; Virginia Haviland is head of the section. Its purpose and scope as a reference and bibliographic service for all interested in children and their literature is described in *Serving Those Who Serve Children*.[11] Old and rare children's books are in the Rare Books Division, which has a valuable collection of Americana but also includes notable British books and, by gift, a collection of Kiplingiana collected by William C. Carpenter and the Jean Hershott collection of Anderseniana and early magazines for children. The Children's Book Section is responsible for the reference service and makes recommendations for purchase, searches for gaps in the collection, and prepares bibliographies. A major and extremely useful work is *Children's Literature : A Guide to Reference Sources* which was published by the Library of Congress in 1966.[12] Foreign books are acquired by exchange or purchased by local agents.

Britain badly needs a reference and information service for research students, publishers and all interested in literature for children, but it should not be considered the responsibility of such a centre to provide book lists and information which should be within the scope of the public library. It is to be hoped that it could co-ordinate work carried out by librarians and others from all over the country so that there would be no unnecessary duplication of effort and other worthwhile projects might be attempted. It should also liaise with other national bodies abroad and with international bodies.

In Sweden there is a central bureau, the Bibliotekstjänst, Lund, Sweden, founded in 1951 by the Swedish Library Association. The Board of Education is represented and it has a school library department. It supplies bound books with printed catalogue cards and also supplies furniture and fittings. Lisa-Christina Persson is head of a staff who arrange courses and workshops and produce book lists and other bibliographical tools. The Bibliotekstjanst has published the IFLA *Library Service to Children*, vols. 1 and 2,[13] and members of IFLA must be grateful for the work of Swedish, Dutch and Danish bureaux on their behalf.

In Holland *Bureau, Boek en Jeugd der C.V.* (Bureau, Book and Youth), founded in 1952, is an information service on children's books and libraries. It is financed by the Netherlands Government and is a section of the Central Association for Public Libraries. It prepares stock lists for the setting up of new libraries, bearing in mind the budget available and the particular needs of the community. It has close liaison with publishers and booksellers and a book-reviewing scheme is organized so that every book published is reviewed by librarians in two different areas. Monthly meetings are held in eleven centres, usually with a member of the bureau staff, to discuss books sent by Bureau, Book and Youth and written reviews are returned to the centre. These are finally sent out in duplicate form to all children's librarians, schools and educational journals. The Bureau also publishes book lists, organizes exhibitions and was responsible for the bibliography, *Professional Literature on Library Work With Children* (1966) which covers sixteen countries.[14]

Bibliotekscentralen is responsible for the publication of the *Dansk Bogfortegnelse* (the Danish national bibliography), the selection of titles for centralized cataloguing for public libraries, and titles to be offered through the centralized binding service, *Indbindingscentralen.*

Each children's book is reviewed by a school librarian and a children's librarian. Reviews and order forms are sent weekly to subscribing libraries and *Indbindingscentralen* supplies books to libraries through local bookshops. The United Kingdom needs a similar national reviewing scheme with reviews available for books as published which could be incorporated in a National Centre for children's literature.

The Youth Libraries Group Committee also made suggestions to improve the British National Bibliography's treatment of children's books.[15] The suggestions were that children's books should be listed as a separate sequence and that the weekly list and annual cumulation should be available as separate items. The index should indicate which are children's books. It was felt that some simplification was needed in the length of the classification number and the form of entry, and that brief annotation indicating age-range, scope and standard should be included.

If a national book-reviewing scheme was established and reviews were available on publication there would not appear to be the same need for this annotation. If entries and class numbers were simplified more schools and libraries would probably use BNB cards but it may be only a matter of time before the stocks of children's, and possibly school, libraries are placed on computer catalogues.

In the United States the Center for Children's Books at the University of Chicago publishes a critical and evaluative review in a monthly bulletin. There is a committee of librarians and subject specialists and teachers who contribute. Books are graded according to school grades and there is also a symbol to indicate assessment. Other reviews appear in the *Horn Book* and in the professional press; in Canada they appear in the Toronto Public Libraries' subscription service.

The Children's Book Council is an association of American Children's Book Editors who co-operate with librarians on book lists and produce a quarterly bulletin, *The Calendar*, giving details of new books of special significance and forthcoming events.

The United States Committee for UNICEF have sponsored an Information Center on Children's Culture with particular interest in countries sponsored by the United Nations Children's Fund. It has books, pamphlets, periodicals, films and sound recordings for and about children in the English language and natively produced books. Anne Pellowski, the compiler of *The World of Children's Literature*,[16] is the Director.

The history of the International Youth Library is described by Jella Lepman, the founder, in *A Bridge of Children's Books*.[17] She describes how it evolved from her concern after the Second World War for the children of Germany who had been deprived of literature during the Nazi régime. An international exhibition of children's books to foster understanding through books was held in Munich in 1946 and was also taken to other German cities. The International Youth Library was founded in Munich in 1949 and made an associated project of UNESCO in 1953; originally it was hoped to have branches in other cities throughout the world. It was founded with large grants from the Rockefeller Foundation and also with help from the American Library Association and the Bavarian Government. It is now supported by the Federal Government, the state of Bavaria and the city of Munich and has a stock of approximately 140,000 volumes, and is fully described by Stephen M. Churchward in the *Library Association Record*, November 1968.[18]

The language stock is in five main sections – German, French, English, Scandinavian and Slavic – but other languages like Dutch, Afrikaans, Spanish and Italian are well represented. There is a librarian responsible for each main group who will liaise with cultural organizations and publishers in his area and arrange exhibitions which travel abroad and are useful for comparative studies.

As a bibliographical centre it has built up a comprehensive stock on children's literature, printing, publishing, illustrating, and librarianship since this section began in 1960. Unobtainable books have been photocopied and there is a newscutting file under countries, and professional periodicals from varying countries. There are eight grants based on the cost of living which are available to non-German nationals for periods of three months to study a chosen project in literature for children or international librarianship.

There is also a lending library with facilities available for any children living in Munich. This has 6,000 volumes, mainly duplicates of the national collections, and includes books in German, French, Italian and English with a separate room for picture books. Activities include language courses in English and French and book discussion groups, and there are classes in the Art Studio under the direction of a specialist teacher.

The UNESCO Collection of Children's Books which was at the International Bureau of Education, Geneva, is now in the International Youth Library. The books mainly cover the period 1920–39 and are in fifty languages.

The International Institute of Children's, Juvenile and Popular Literature was founded in Vienna in 1965 and is a research institute and documentation centre concerned with children's literature and its business aspects. It also advises on international research projects and arranges conferences, seminars and exhibitions. In joint co-operation with the International Board on Books for Young People it publishes *Bookbird*.

The foundation of the International Board on Books for Young People was approved at a conference in 1951 and developed under the leadership of Jella Lepman from her work at the International Youth Library. Although Zurich was originally chosen for the site, it was finally established in Vienna. Its first task was concerned with horror comics; today it is interested in the effects of other media – films, radio, television and periodicals on children's reading. Its functions are to co-ordinate organizations in other countries with international interest in children's books, to found institutes for investigation of children's and youth literature and to work closely with the International Youth Library. It advises on translations of books through its national sections with the aim of fostering understanding through books and introducing outstanding books to children of other countries.

In 1956 the Hans Christian Andersen Award was made for the first time by the International Board on Books for Young People. The first recipient was Eleanor Farjeon. It is awarded bi-annually at the Board's congress not for a particular book but to a living writer whose complete works have made a contribution to literature for children. In 1966 a second award was inaugurated for the complete works of an illustrator. Britain now has an informal body of interested individuals who are making recommendations for these awards. A problem in making the Hans Christian Andersen Award is that some books will have to be read in translation by the judges and apart from the difficulties this presents, some excellent books have a national appeal which is uneasily uprooted. Illustration has a more international appeal and at the biennale of Book Illustration in Bratislava prizes are awarded internationally for illustration in sixteen groups. Every country is asked to send the work of twenty artists for the exhibition and competition.

Many countries make their own awards and rules of eligibility vary considerably. The American Library Association awards the Newbery Medal to the most distinguished book for children of the previous year and the Caldecott Medal, which is of more limited scope than the British Kate Greenaway Award, to the most distinguished picture book.

The Mildred L. Batchelder Award encourages excellence in the translation of children's books as it is awarded to the American publisher of a children's book originally produced in another country and later published in the United States. Another American prize is the Laura Ingalls Wilder Award which is presented every five years to an author or illustrator who has made a lasting contribution to literature for children.

In Britain, apart from the Library Association Medals, the *Guardian* has made an annual award since 1966 for a children's book selected by their literary editor and critics, and *The Times Educational Supplement* since 1972 for an information book. A list of prize-winning books is available called *Preisgekrönte Kinderbucher*. It is compiled at the International Youth Library and is available in hardback or paperback.[19]

UNESCO has since 1966 made a considerable contribution to developing library services to children overseas in Asia, Africa and Latin America, where possible through a public library scheme. Demonstration libraries have been set up, mobile libraries have been organized, seminars have been held and experienced librarians have gone to advise on new services. Teacher/librarian courses have been held and through UNESCO Fellowships local staff have been able to receive experience and training in more developed countries. UNESCO publishes the *Unesco Bulletin for Libraries* bi-monthly and commissioned Lionel R. McColvin to write *Public Library Services for Children* from an international standpoint.[20] Another manual which it sponsored was *The Primary School Library and Its Services* by Mary P. Douglas.[21] Other publications include *Books for Asian Children*, a selective list of publications from world literature suitable for use in Asia in the original, translation or adaptation, as an aid to governments, publishers, school and public libraries.[22]

The International Federation of Library Associations (IFLA), founded in 1927, is an international body which holds annual congresses and endeavours to exchange ideas and information. The Library Work With Children, established in 1959, is a sub-section of the Public Libraries section and another sub-section deals with hospital libraries. Its publishing programme has included *Library Service to Children*, volumes 1 and 2, covering conditions in twenty-six countries;[23] volume one gives a memorandum on basic principles of library work with children. Volume two includes an article by M. Joy Lewis, 'The Hospital Librarian and the Child', and a bibliography on this subject. The Public Library Section has published *Library Service to Young Adults*[24] and the sub-section *Translations of Children's Books*, edited by Lisa-Christina Persson and published in 1962, which discusses difficulties of translations, especially in countries with a small output in their own language, and recommends books for translation from sixteen countries.[25]

The bibliography on literature of children's library work[26] was compiled in 1966 from contributions from member countries and from May 1973 *Children's Literature Abstracts* is to be published quarterly by the Library Work with Children sub-section of the IFLA. This should prove invaluable as material is often difficult to locate. The chairman, Mrs Aase Bredsdorf of the Danish Library Inspectorate, and Mrs Lisa-Christina Persson of Bibliotekstjänst, Sweden, maintain a record of designated correspondents to communicate with on IFLA matters in other countries and they in turn provide a link between organizations in their own countries and others through IFLA.

International co-operation in children's literature is also taking place through the Loughborough School of Librarianship International Summer Schools held in Loughborough, Europe and America. Continental and British librarians have had the opportunity to welcome American librarians and teachers to their libraries through the Oklahoma University Library Schools, while library schools and professional bodies run foreign study tours. The Colombo Plan, UNESCO Fellowships and internship schemes in different countries have given opportunities for training and a mutual exchange of ideas and information, and librarians have gone out to work in developing countries for a few years leaving local qualified staff to run the service. Short advisory tours for senior librarians are also organized by UNESCO and the British Council.

Librarians working with children and books cannot afford to be complacent. They must be aware how much more needs to be accomplished in their own area, country and overseas. Co-operation is essential at home and with international agencies, librarians and teachers abroad, so that free access to a wide range of books for knowledge and pleasure is recognized as an inherent right of children everywhere.

REFERENCES

1 Janet Hill (ed.). *Books for Children: the Homelands of Immigrants to Britain.* London, Institute of Race Relations (Special Series), 1971.
2 *An Investigation into the Physical Wear and Length of Life of Books for Young Children, 1967–1969.* Pamphlet no. 6. London, Library Association, Youth Libraries Group, 1970.
3 Dorothy K. Robertson. *The Reviewing of Children's Books in Britain.* Pamphlet no. 4. London, Library Association, Youth Libraries Group, 1969.
4 *Book Selection for Children.* Pamphlet no. 3. London, Library Association Youth Libraries Group, 1969.
5 A selection including *Buy, Beg or Borrow? A Choice of Books for Children* compiled by Kenneth Wood. Pamphlet no. 5. London, Library Association, Youth Libraries Group, 1969.
Into Space, compiled by Malcolm Neesam. Storylines no. 2., London Library Association, Youth Libraries Group, 1972.
6 'A National Centre for Children's Literature – A Symposium': (1) 'Services for Children Offered by the British Museum' by J. A. D. Townsend, and (2) 'A National Centre for Children's Literature' by B. W. Alderson. In *Proceedings of the Public Libraries Conference Held at Brighton, 1968.* London, Library Association, 1968. pp. 64–71.
7 *The Osborne Collection of Early Children's Books, 1566–1910: A Catalogue. Prepared . . . by Judith St. John.* Toronto Public Libraries, 1958.
8 *A Chronicle of Boys' and Girls' House and A Selected List of Recent Additions to the Osborne Collection of Early Children's Books 1542–1910 and the Lillian H. Smith Collection 1911–1963.* Toronto Public Libraries, 1964
9 Salway, Lance (ed.). *Special Collections of Children's Literature: A Guide to Collections in Libraries and Other Organisations in London and the Home Counties.* Pamphlet no. 11. London, Library Association, Youth Libraries Group, 1972.
10 Frances Clarke-Sayers. *Children's Books in the Library of Congress.* Washington, 1952.
11 Virginia Haviland. 'Serving Those Who Serve Children; A National Reference Library of Children's Books'. *Quarterly Journal of the Library of Congress,* vol. 22, October 1965. pp. 301–16.
12 *Children's Literature: A Guide to Reference Sources. Prepared under the Direction of Virginia Haviland.* Washington, Library of Congress, 1966.
13 International Federation of Library Associations. Committee on Library Work with Children. *Library Service to Children,* vol. 1, edited by Eileen Colwell, and vol. 2, edited by Lisa-Christina Persson. Lund, Sweden, Bibliotekstjänst, 1966.
14 International Federation of Library Associations. Subsection on Library Work with Children. Bibliography: *Professional Literature on Library Work with Children,* compiled by Annie Moerkercken Van der Meulin. IFLA, The Hague, 1966.

15 British National Bibliography. 'Suggestions Arising Out of Meetings between Representatives of the Y.L.G. and Mr. Wells at B.N.B.' *Youth Library Group News*, vol. 14, no. 1, February 1970.

16 Anne Pellowski. *The World of Children's Literature*. New York, Bowker, 1968.

17 Jella Lepman. *A Bridge of Children's Books*. London and Chicago, Brockhampton Press and American Library Association, 1969.

18 Stephen M. Churchward. 'Twenty Years of the International Youth Library'. *Library Association Record*, vol. 70, November 1968. pp. 280–2.

19 *Preisgekrönte Kinderbucher* (Children's Prize Books). Translated into English by Walter Scherf. Munich and Berlin, Verlag Documentation, 1969.

20 Lionel R. McColvin. *Public Library Services for Children*. Paris, UNESCO, 1957.

21 Mary P. Douglas. *The Primary School Library and Its Services*. UNESCO Manuals for Libraries, no. 12. Paris, UNESCO, 1961.

22 Shakuntala Bhatawdekar (comp.). *Books for Asian Children*. Paris, UNESCO, 1956.

23 See note 13 above.

24 Emma Cohn and Brita Olsson (eds.). *Library Service to Young Adults*. Published by the Public Libraries Section of IFLA. Copenhagen, Bibliotekscentralen, 1968.

25 Lisa-Christina Persson (ed.). *Translations of Children's Books*. Lund, Sweden, Bibliotekstjänst, 1962.

26 See note 14 above.

FURTHER READING

Bredsdorff, Aase. 'International Federation of Library Associations'. Subsection on Library Work with Children. 'Report on Activities 1955–1967', *International Library Review*, vol. 3, no. 11, January 1971. pp. 35–49.

Ellis, Alec. *How To Find Out about Children's Literature*. 2nd edition. Oxford, Pergamon, 1968.

Townsend, John Rowe. 'Where Do Children's Books Stand?'. *Growing Point*, vol. 6, no. 6, December 1967, and vol. 7, no. 1, March 1968.

Index

Specific titles referred to in the text will be found in the lists of recommended books after the relevant chapter.